Cheshire MURDERS

Alan Hayhurst

First published in 2006 by
Sutton Publishing Limited

Reprinted in 2009 by
The History Press
The Mill, Brimscombe Port,
Stroud, Gloucestershire, GL5 2QG
www.thehistorypress.co.uk

Reprinted 2010, 2011

British Library Cataloguing in Publication Data
A catalogue record for this book is available from the British Library.

ISBN 978-0-7509-4076-4

Typeset in 10.5/13.5pt Sabon.
Typesetting and origination by
Sutton Publishing.
Printed and bound in Great Britain by
Marston Book Services Limited, Didcot

CONTENTS

ACKNOWLEDGEMENTS

The author wishes to thank the following for their help in the researching of this book: Janet Easner and Philip Coops, who were kind enough to share with me their thoughts about the Mary Malpas case; Fiona Orr, who kindly lent me her precious copy of *George Chapman*, in the Notable British Trials series; Anne Loader for her help with illustrations and permission to quote from one of her publications; John Moffatt of the Friends of Flaybrick for his invaluable help with the Lock Ah Tam case and Fa Chen, Chairman of the British and Chinese Children's Society, for his translation of the tombstone inscription; Terry Harding, who introduced me to Christine Clough of the Friends of Gorse Hall and for her enthusiastic assistance; Alan and Marie Elmer; Stewart Evans, Sarah Bryce, Helen Bradbury, Alison Miles and the team at Sutton Publishing; and the staff at the National Archives, Kew, the Liverpool and Chester Record Offices, the Congleton Museum, Lymm Library and Tameside Local Studies & Archive Centre, who were generous with their time. If I have left anyone out, I apologise, but you know who you are.

As ever, I owe a considerable debt to my wife, who once again put up with my virtual absence for a year, cloistered in the office upstairs, and who made countless cups of coffee and refrained from complaining about the state of the lawns.

INTRODUCTION

The county of Cheshire has a long and honourable history and like many others has changed its boundaries frequently over the years, although all the cases in this book have a real connection with the county. Mainly agricultural, there are few large centres of population, which at first sight makes it a poor subject for a true crime history; but as I carried out my research, I quickly came to realise that Sherlock Holmes was correct when he told Dr Watson, 'It is my belief, founded upon my experience, that the lowest and vilest alleys of London do not present a more dreadful record of sin than does the smiling and beautiful countryside.'

Some of the cases in this book are better known than others, such as the inexplicable shooting of his wife and two daughters by Lock Ah Tam in 1926 and the Gorse Hall murder of 1909, which still excites aficionados of true crime and those who like a good unsolved mystery. Lesser-known cases include the mysterious murder of Mary Malpas in 1835 (my theory about who really did kill young Mary at Doddington has, I think, not been seen in print before) and the crime of Frederick George Wood in Bramhall, 1922, a classic example of the pointless murder, for little or no reward. Finally, few outside the town have ever heard the tale of the 'Congleton Cannibal'.

In order to ensure that the facts are as accurate as possible, I have spent many hours in the National Archive at Kew and the Record Offices of Chester and Liverpool, poring over depositions, transcripts and other documents, and struggling to read the pages of contemporary newspapers, many of which boast print sizes so small that they defy all but the largest magnifying-glass. Lastly, I have tried not to put words into the mouths of the people concerned, unless I have been able to confirm them from sources mentioned above.

1
THE CONGLETON CANNIBAL

Congleton, 1776

The church of St Peter, Congleton, situated on a ridge to the south-west of the modern town centre, is a fine example of eighteenth-century design. Almost opposite, a small street named Priesty Fields runs down to a valley, in the bottom of which is a small stream known as the Howty Brook. A path runs along the banks of the brook, connecting Congleton to the village of Astbury, just over a mile away, where stands the church of St Mary, historically the mother church of Congleton and one of the finest parish churches in Cheshire. The locals have used the Howty Brook path to travel between the two townships for centuries and the path is still there today, in places overarched by trees and no doubt looking much as it did 200 years ago. The brook itself seems innocuous, being much overgrown by vegetation, but in bad weather it was formerly prone to flooding causing, as Robert Head wrote in his *Congleton Past and Present*, 'much destruction of property'.

Among the parishioners of Astbury St Mary's in 1776 was Samuel Thorley, aged 52, a large, rough man of limited intelligence and short temper, whom the local people preferred to leave very much alone if they could. A newspaper of the time, the *Chester Courant*, said of him, 'In general, he was looked upon as a man of furious temper and dangerous to affront, or banter.'

Thorley worked as gravedigger at St Mary's, and to eke out his meagre existence he was also a part-time butcher in Congleton. He was said to take a great delight in his butchering trade and it was rumoured that he had also developed a taste for raw meat, although this could have had more to do with his lack of money than any appetite for blood. On occasion he was known to sleep rough, but when he could afford the rent he lodged with Hannah Oakes, a widow who lived in a small, tumbledown thatched cottage near the Howty Brook.

On Saturday 23 November 1776 a local farmer, Newman Garside, was herding his cows into a field alongside the brook and, having settled them, walked down to the stream to enjoy a pipe of his favourite tobacco. Two young boys were with him, and one of them, 13-year-old William

Path between Congleton and Astbury. (Author)

Barrett, noticed what appeared to be a woman's cloak, made of blue material, floating in an eddy near the bank of the stream.

He pointed this out to Garside, who encouraged the lad to risk a ducking and retrieve the cloak, which he did with some difficulty. Hidden underneath it in the water was another garment, which young William also retrieved. Dumping both pieces of cloth onto the bank, he stretched them out. The second piece, yellow in colour, bore several reddish stains; and although these meant nothing to the boy, his employer thought he knew a bloodstain when he saw one and examined the garment closely. Satisfied that he was right, and seeing two farm-hands in the adjoining field, he gestured for them to come over.

Humphrey Newton and John Beswick ran down to where Garside stood, holding the wet cloth. 'It looks like blood', he said, rubbing his fingers against the stains. The two farm-hands were not immediately convinced, but urged on by Garside they joined the two boys in searching the area and in a short time they had discovered quite a collection of articles, including a cap; a black ribbon; a small bag, which held a half-eaten brown loaf, an old tobacco box, a thimble and a pair of scissors; two song sheets; a sewing bag containing needles and thread; and a woman's petticoat. Suddenly, John Beswick exclaimed in horror as he stared into the stream and saw what appeared to be human limbs floating in the water.

Garside immediately sent the two boys scurrying to fetch the local constable, John Martin, who soon came running down to the brook followed by a crowd of curious villagers. Once Garside had stuttered out his story, Martin organised a more thorough search, which quickly produced more human remains, including a head that was obviously female and a woman's breast. Whoever had cut up the dead girl's body had made a thorough job of it; but even so, the remains were soon identified as belonging to Annie Smith, a girl in her early twenties. Annie scraped a living by selling ballad sheets, which were popular as a means of entertainment at the time, and also, it was rumoured, was not averse to selling herself to those who could pay a few coppers for the privilege.

The following day, Sunday, the remains were retrieved from a local barn where they had been placed overnight, and the local inhabitants crowded round to view the grisly findings, which even with decomposition rapidly setting in were still recognisable. A grave was dug at Congleton St Peter's and the remains were hastily interred, after which an inquest was held and promptly suspended *sine die*.

A local weaver, Thomas Cordwell, while walking near the Howty Brook that morning had passed three men talking, one of whom he had recognised

St Mary's churchyard, Astbury, where Samuel Thorley acted as gravedigger. (Author)

The Howty Brook, Congleton. (Author)

as Samuel Thorley. The gravedigger and part-time butcher had appeared agitated, and Cordwell had heard him insisting in a loud voice to his companions that he had known nothing about the murder until the body parts were discovered. This set Cordwell thinking; and he was still pondering the subject when he arrived home for lunch, where his wife was waiting to tell him the latest gossip.

The whole town was agog with the events of the past two days and the popular view placed Samuel Thorley at the top of the list of suspects for the terrible crime, although, as is usually the case with gossip, facts were scarce and most of it was tittle-tattle and rumour. It was really nothing more than Thorley's bad temper and his rough skill with a butcher's knife that had prompted the villagers to point the finger of suspicion at him, but Cordwell continued to mull over the morning's events, becoming more sure in his own mind as the day went on that Thorley had indeed got something to do with the death of Annie Smith. He decided to look for Thorley, in order to examine him for traces of blood. However, the suspect was nowhere to be found, so together with a friend, Thomas Elkin, Cordwell went back to the Howty Brook. While walking along the bank, they saw what appeared to be bloodstains on a stile over a pathway that led to Hannah Oakes's cottage. Hannah was standing at her door as the two men approached and they stopped to tell her about the bloodstains. The old woman replied by saying that for the past five days Thorley had been lodging with her. On the evening of the murder, he had arrived home wearing his butcher's apron, in which he was carrying some meat that he claimed had been given to him in exchange for his butchering services, when a pig belonging to a local farmer had died suddenly. He was soaked through and in reply to his landlady's questioning explained that he had fallen into the Howty Brook on his way home, but luckily had been able to prevent the meat from being swept away by the swollen stream.

Thorley had asked the old woman to boil the meat immediately, but Hannah had already prepared something for the evening meal and had stubbornly declined to do any more cooking that day, despite Thorley's obvious displeasure.

The next evening, 21 November, Thorley brushed the old woman's objections aside and boiled the meat himself, Mrs Oakes commenting that it looked a bit 'off' to her and that she would eat none of it. Her lodger sat down at the table with a bowl of the meat in front of him and started to wolf it down, but he had barely got through the first mouthful when he rushed to the door and was violently sick outside. Returning, he told her brusquely to get rid of the rest of the meat as it was unfit, but despite her own initial misgivings and Thorley's sickness, Mrs Oakes could not bear to see 'good' food thrown away and she decided to boil some of the meat for fat, keeping the rest of it in the cold oven. It beggars belief that Hannah should have kept the remaining pieces to eat later, especially since the previous boiling had obviously not prevented the meat from rotting, but it has to be remembered that in the eighteenth century rotten meat was the norm for most poor people, who had to manage with whatever food they could scavenge.

Now thoroughly alarmed, Thomas Cordwell asked to see what was left of the meat and, to his horror, noticed that one piece looked remarkably like a human calf. Hannah Oakes's face turned ashen. 'He told me it was pork!' she cried. The old woman was more than willing for Cordwell to take the meat away and he immediately took it to the police, who called in a doctor to examine it further. The doctor had no doubt that this was human flesh, and matched the pieces that had already been found.

The inquest on Annie Smith was hastily resumed and this new evidence was put before the court, Mrs Oakes then testifying that Thorley had told her that he was going to pick up the pay that was owing to him and was going to Leek, some 10 miles away, claiming, 'They are laying the charge of murder on me.' This was enough to induce the jury to bring in a verdict of murder against Thorley and a further search was made, the fugitive eventually being discovered in a cottage at School Lane, Astbury. Constable Martin promptly arrested him and took him off to the cells at Congleton Town Hall, from where he was taken next day to Chester, to await trial.

In those days, judges visited the county only twice a year, and so the unfortunates on remand had often to wait anything up to six months in the dripping wet cells underneath the Chester Castle walls, with little light and no heat. Although there were two beds in each cell, there could be five or six prisoners to share them, so that three or four often had to sleep on the stone floor. No doubt Samuel Thorley, at this stage legally innocent until proved guilty, used his weight and his rough ways to ensure that he was one of the fortunate two with a bed!

The trial took place before Mr Justice Moreton on 3 April 1777. Thorley was apparently overcome by his position: understandably, four months' incarceration had done nothing for his physical and mental state and he made little or no attempt to put up a defence, being unable, according to the law of the day, to give evidence on his own behalf under oath. The jury had no difficulty in finding him guilty, and he was sentenced to be hanged and then displayed in chains on the gibbet. The sentence was carried out on 10 April and a month later the tarred and manacled corpse was exhibited near Priesty Fields for the amusement of the community, who took the opportunity to have a field day, the boys from the local Grammar School being given a special half-holiday to view the spectacle!

The *Chester Courant* reported that Thorley had shown 'no remorse for his terrible crime and met his death with indifference'. In the local taverns, the inhabitants of Congleton regaled themselves for many weeks afterwards with tales of the 'Congleton Cannibal'; there were even some who claimed to have purchased pieces of 'pork' from the executed man.

More than 100 years later, Robert Head noted in his *Congleton, Past and Present*, a valued copy of which is kept in the Congleton Museum, that 'Samuel Thorley, a butcher's follower at Congleton, was executed at Chester for the murder of Ann Smith, a ballad singer aged 22', and went on to say, 'It will never be known what led to the horrible fate of Ann Smith.' However, Head does venture to suggest that the young ballad-singer had stolen a knife from Thorley, which he had used to kill her after chasing her along the banks of the stream.

In the Register of Burials for St Peter's Church, possibly many years later, someone wrote after the name of the dead girl, 'A woman that was murdered by Samuel Thorley'.

St Peter's, Congleton, where Annie Smith lies in an unmarked grave. (Author)

2

DEATH IN THE DINGLE

Lymm, 1798–1901

The church of St Mary stands on an elevated position above the township of Lymm, a few miles from the bustling market town of Altrincham. The rector in 1797 was the Revd Peter Egerton Leigh, who was also the Archdeacon of Salop and a member of an old and respected family in the area. Down the hill, a few hundred yards away from the church, was the rectory, a substantial black and white house in which Egerton Leigh lived with his wife, Theodosia, and which was perched on the side of a deep ravine known locally as 'The Dingle'. This valley was well planted with specimen trees, through which tumbled a lively stream emerging at the 'Lower Dam', which today still makes a pleasant feature in the centre of Lymm village, only yards away from the ancient Market Cross.

Egerton Leigh lived in some style, and was able to employ several servants including a butler, John Thornhill, a popular young man in the village, born in the Cotswolds in 1769. John was a tall, good-looking young man, proud of his position, who always took great pains to dress well. However, he was not over-endowed with brains and could be inclined to violence if people did not offer him the respect to which he felt he was entitled. He had been at the rectory for some seven years and was engaged to be married to Mrs Egerton Leigh's maid, Rebecca Clark, a liaison which met with the wholehearted approval of his employers.

On the face of it, John and his Rebecca had a lot to look forward to – secure, relatively well-paid jobs, good accommodation and a certain position in the local community which could stand them in good stead, should they ever decide to move on. It is therefore a puzzle why, in the spring of 1797, John should have allowed himself to jeopardise all this by getting involved with a local woman, Sally Statham. Sally took in washing to make ends meet and had two children, a son John, aged 13, and a much younger daughter. Additionally, she was twenty years older than Thornhill and was described locally as 'large and lusty', a description that fitted her to a tee.

The old cross at Lymm, which John Thornhill would have passed many times. (Author)

Lymm church and Upper Dam. (Author's collection)

It was not possible to keep such a liaison secret in the small community, especially when the rector's butler enjoyed such a high profile, and rumours soon began to circulate. In the early summer, the rector, his family and the servants went to Lichfield, where Egerton Leigh had church duties to perform, and by the time they returned, in October, the news was out that Sally was pregnant and that John Thornhill was the father. One of Rebecca's 'friends' could not wait to tell her the news as soon as she returned, and the poor girl, overcome with shame and the possible loss of her fiancé, faced up to Thornhill and a terrific row ensued. Thornhill denied being the father of Sally's child and said that the best way to sort things out would be for the two of them to confront Statham after church on the following Sunday. This they did, going to her house and insisting that they should come in to discuss the matter. To Rebecca's relief, Sally denied that John was the father of her child or that he had been having an affair with her. The couple then left; although Rebecca might not have been feeling so pleased if she had known that her John had already seen Sally earlier in the day and had had a long and earnest conversation with her.

However, this was not the end of the matter. Sally had lied to get herself temporarily out of an awkward confrontation, but afterwards could not resist boasting that Thornhill was indeed the father of her soon-to-be-born baby and consequently the rumours began to circulate again. This put the young man in a very awkward spot, for if he were to be named as the father, both Sally and Rebecca could sue him for breach of promise, and in addition he would be forced by the parish to support the baby and its mother. Ultimately, the scandal would result in dismissal from his position at the rectory, and his chances of getting another job with the same pay and prospects were virtually nil.

Had he kept calm and denied Sally's story, he might just have got away with it. There was no way in which paternity could be ascertained in those days, and Statham had a certain reputation among the young men of the town which might have been sufficient to cast doubt on any claims that she had made. However, time was short and John did not relish another angry row with his fiancée. He discussed the matter with his friend John Parr, a gardener at the rectory, who gave him the benefit of his advice: 'I would give her a few pounds and send her back to her own parish!'

On 5 January 1798, Thornhill arranged to meet Sally in The Dingle, a place that would afford them some privacy while they discussed ways out of their joint dilemma. Statham, who was now less than four weeks from delivering her baby, was eager in the extreme to have things settled, and, to her mind, the simplest and most effective solution would be for Thornhill to marry her immediately.

This was not exactly what John had in mind, and whatever discussions took place by the waterside resulted in the badly beaten body of Sally Statham being flung into the stream, where it was discovered floating in the Lower Dam the following day. The body was examined by two doctors from nearby Knutsford, who were of the opinion that Sally had been dead, or nearly so, when she was thrown into the water and that wounds to her head had been caused by blows from a hammer. They also commented on the signs of imminent childbirth, the fact of which was in any event now common knowledge in Lymm. Thornhill was summoned before the rector, who demanded to know what had happened and why some of his clothing appeared to be bloodstained. The butler's first story was that he had gone into the yard to drive off some pigs and had fallen over the cinders, but as this did not satisfy his employer he changed his tale and claimed that he had fallen in the dark when going to the privy while carrying a large burning coal to light his way.

This account met with no better reception than the first, and the rector made it clear that he knew the truth of the matter. Thornhill sobbed, 'Nobody saw me. How can they hurt me?', and pleaded with the rector to hide him. 'That I cannot do, John', said his employer, and walked away.

The now terrified Thornhill demanded to see Mrs Egerton Leigh, and it is said that when she clapped eyes on him the fact of his guilt stood out like a beacon and she begged him to give himself up, while he in turn begged her to give him the chance to escape. 'Nobody saw me', he repeated, but to no avail. Realising that he was in more danger as the minutes went by, he decided to make a run for it, but he was too well known in the area and before nightfall he had been caught and detained overnight at the Spread Eagle Hotel.

The security arrangements at the hotel evidently left a lot to be desired as Thornhill managed to escape his captors after breakfast next morning.

However, it was not long before he was captured again and deposited in the far more effective cells at Chester Castle.

The trial began on Friday 29 April 1798 in the presence of two judges, Francis Burton and James Adair. The evidence against the accused was largely that of his fellow servants at the rectory, who had seen him on the night of the murder covered in blood. It is unclear why this young man should not have taken steps to keep himself free from gore, or to cover it with a cloak until he could change his clothing, but the servants had also noticed that he had burnt his hand and that both his appearance and manner were suspicious. He had given conflicting accounts of how his hand had come to be blistered, although as the dead woman had obviously been bludgeoned to death this might have been irrelevant. His defence, seemingly born from panic at his situation and without any real hope of success, was to hold out to the court that as no one had seen him commit the crime, he could not be found guilty; and he persisted with this claim throughout the hearing. The judges wasted little time in handing down the death sentence and only two days later he was on the gallows at Boughton, just over a mile away from the scene of the trial and the traditional local venue for hangings, where he confessed at the last moment. Sally Statham was laid to rest in the churchyard at Lymm, as was the rector, who died only six months later, although whether this tragedy had anything to do with Thornhill's death is not recorded.

Hard by the entrance to the church at Lymm is a well-worn tombstone, now slightly leaning, the engravings on it difficult to read. It is the grave plot of the Taylor family, who were farmers in the area. Elizabeth Taylor (known as 'Bessie'), the daughter of Thomas Parsonage Taylor, was born in 1864 and spent the first twenty years of her life working for her father. Becoming disenchanted with her lot – her father was reluctant to pay her more than subsistence wages – and also perhaps with the lack of marriageable men in Lymm, she set off for London and soon obtained work as a domestic servant and later as a restaurant manageress. She was a well-built young woman, of medium height, heavy-busted, with a thick crop of frizzy hair.

Early in 1898, Bessie Taylor met the man who was to become her nemesis. She replied to a newspaper advertisement asking for the services of a barmaid-cum-housekeeper, placed by one Severin Klosowski, the son of a Polish carpenter, and by now going under the name of George Chapman. He was a stocky, heavily moustachioed man in his late thirties, with hypnotic eyes and a shock of dark hair, and was now running the Prince of Wales Tavern, in Bartholomew Square.

Whether it was due to his eyes or not is not recorded, but within a short time George proposed to Bessie and they were supposed to have been married one Sunday afternoon in 1898, although a search by the author has failed to reveal the existence of a marriage certificate.

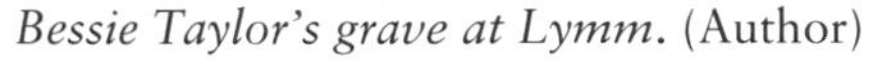

Bessie Taylor's grave at Lymm. (Author)

Bessie Taylor and George Chapman. (Author's collection)

The certificate, in any case, would have been irrelevant, as not only had Chapman a wife in Poland, who had vanished into the mists of time after paying him a brief visit in England, but he had also gone through a marriage ceremony with one Lucy Baderski, the sister of a Polish tailor in Walthamstow (again, no marriage certificate can be found). After a brief sojourn in America, during which he separated from Lucy, Chapman took up hairdressing as a means of earning a living and 'married' a lady named Annie Chapman, who left after a year. Klosowski then adopted her maiden surname and became George Chapman. Matters now took a more serious turn as he embarked on a series of liaisons, each of which resulted in the death of the woman involved. First, in 1895, he supposedly went through a marriage ceremony with Mary Isabella Spink, who was already married to Shadrach Spink and had two children by him. Shadrach had become fed up with her intemperate behaviour and disappeared, but not leaving his wife penniless, as she had inherited the quite large sum of £600 from a relative. This sum, by 1887, had found its way into Chapman's capacious pockets.

He promptly leased a hairdresser's shop in Old Hastings, and as Mary Isabella was quite an accomplished pianist Chapman hired an instrument and his 'musical shaves' quickly became popular in the town. It was about this time that he made the acquaintance of a local pharmacist, Mr Davidson, whom he persuaded to sell to him a quantity of a well-known poison, a salt of antimony called tartar emetic. Soon, Chapman was in possession of more than an ounce of the poison (over 400 grains), the fatal dose of which could be as little as fifteen grains, but had not been able to avoid signing Davidson's poisons book, a matter about which the pharmacist was very particular.

Within weeks, the Chapmans were back in London, having taken the lease of the Prince of Wales Tavern, off the City Road, although this move did not seem to suit Mrs Spinks/Chapman's health, as she began to suffer from severe vomiting attacks and bad stomach pains. These worsened and the unfortunate woman died on the morning of Christmas Day, 1897. Chapman displayed considerable grief at the loss of his 'wife' and the death certificate, signed by Dr Rogers, ascribed the death to phthisis, which usually meant a wasting disease or any debilitating lung or throat infection. It had been noticed by her friends that Mary Chapman had lost a lot of weight before she died, and there were also mutterings when they discovered that she had been laid to rest in a pauper's grave.

It was shortly after this that Bessie Taylor came on the scene. Believing that she was legally married (Chapman seems to have been good at persuading his lady friends that they had gone through a marriage ceremony), Bessie adopted the title of 'Mrs Chapman' but her new position in life did not seem to agree with her, for soon she too went into decline. Formerly a healthy woman, she began to lose weight, but this did not stop Chapman uprooting them again to take on the Grapes at Bishop's Stortford – there seems to have been a glut of licensed premises in need of a landlord at the time!

Chapman's attitude to Bessie also changed and he now became violent and once threatened her with a gun, several of which he had on the premises. A further move back to London found them in charge of the Monument Tavern in Union Street, Borough, but the return to the City did nothing to halt Bessie's decline and she now sought the ministrations of Dr Stoker. He could do nothing, and early on 13 February 1901 Bessie died, death being attributed to 'exhaustion from vomiting and diarrhoea'.

Bessie had kept in touch with her family during her wanderings, and they quickly arranged for her body to be returned to Cheshire and buried in the family grave, her erstwhile husband seemingly having raised no objection (although whether or not he attended the funeral is not recorded). Her mother and father did not long survive her, Thomas Parsonage Taylor passing away on 11 June the following year, aged 65, and his wife following him on 22 August. Bessie's epitaph reads simply, 'Bessie, died February 13 1901, aged 36 years'.

And there the matter might have ended, if George Chapman had not taken one last victim. In August 1901, still landlord of the Monument Tavern, Chapman again sought a barmaid and Maud Marsh answered his advertisement.

The fortunes of Chapman's latest 'wife' followed much the same lines as the others: soon, she was suffering from sickness, vomiting and diarrhoea so badly that she had a short spell in hospital and returned to be treated by Dr Stoker. He was as unable to spot the cause of her condition as he had been with poor Bessie.

Chapman now moved for the final time to the Crown in Union Street, Borough, where Dr Stoker continued to attend Maud. George, ever the solicitous husband, insisted that he should do all the cooking and served Maud her meals himself, even though he had secured the services of a Mrs Toon to help with the nursing.

One day, Chapman left a glass of brandy-and-soda by the bedside of the invalid, but she was too weak to drink it. Mrs Toon and Maud's mother, who had called to see how her daughter was getting on, decided to share the liquid between them and were soon having painful attacks of vomiting and diarrhoea themselves. Mr Marsh and one of his daughters were now also in attendance, and during a family conference Marsh proposed that he should refer the matter to his own doctor without telling Maud's husband what he proposed to do.

Somewhat to Chapman's angry surprise, a Dr Grapel arrived to examine Maud, accompanied by Dr Stoker, and the observant Grapel, unlike his colleague, who had no suspicions of anything, soon diagnosed slow poisoning and decided that it must be arsenic. Before he and Stoker could take any remedial action, Maud died suddenly and the two medical men stubbornly refused to sign a death certificate without a post-mortem, which Stoker performed himself. Initially, he found nothing to account for the death of his patient, but he took the precaution of removing the stomach and contents and sending them to the Chemical Research Association, where Richard Bodmer, an analyst, quickly reported the presence of arsenic. Stoker at once informed the police.

Chapman was arrested on Saturday 25 October 1902 and charged with the murder of Maud Marsh. Among his effects, the police found nearly £300 in gold and notes, an enormous sum for a wandering tavern-keeper to have amassed, and some 'white powders'. They also discovered Chapman's real identity. At Maud's funeral, which Chapman was not permitted to attend, he was represented by a wreath with the 'In Memoriam' card marked simply, 'From a devoted friend G.C.', which he had actually written while standing in the dock at the police court. That hearing was quickly adjourned while the bodies of Bessie Taylor and Mary Spink were exhumed, and on its resumption Chapman was committed for trial at the Central Criminal Court.

The trial began on 11 February 1903 in front of Mr Justice Grantham, not a very auspicious choice of judge so far as the accused was concerned, as Grantham had the unnerving habit of making his mind up as to the guilt or otherwise of the accused well before all the evidence had been given, a decision that he did not attempt to shield from the jury.

The evidence against Chapman was almost overwhelming, including that of Dr Thomas Stevenson, who testified that he had examined the exhumed body of Bessie 'Chapman', as the plate on the coffin named her, and had found nearly thirty grains of tartar emetic in the corpse, which was extremely well preserved, a known effect of the poison. No evidence was called for the defence and the closing speech by Mr George Elliott lasted barely more than 4 minutes. The summing-up by Mr Justice Grantham was a travesty of what a good summing-up should be, being clearly weighted against the accused, and after that it was hardly surprising that it took the jury only 11 minutes to find Chapman guilty.

Mr Justice Grantham. (Author's collection)

The only question that remains is Chapman's motive. His succession of wives appears to have brought him little benefit and he was rarely short of money. However, he appears to have had an uncontrollable lust for women, which turned equally quickly to disgust and a need to remove them from the scene.

After conviction, Chapman was confined in Wandsworth Prison and after an appeal to the Home Secretary for clemency brought the inevitable refusal, he was executed on 7 April 1903 by William Billington.

After his death, Chapman gained even more notoriety by being suspected of being the Whitechapel killer, 'Jack the Ripper', the mysterious serial killer, never caught, who was held to be responsible for at least five killings in 1888. Chapman had almost certainly been in the Whitechapel area at the relevant time, but all his killings were by means of poison, while those of 'Jack' were by the knife, which in the view of the author makes it extremely unlikely that the two series of murders are connected.

History has it that Bessie's grave in Lymm churchyard became a place of pilgrimage for those attracted by the notoriety which attached to Chapman after his execution, and the crowds greatly disturbed the vicar, Mr Thurston, who had the name 'Chapman' erased from the headstone.

3

MURDER MISTAKEN?

Doddington, 1835

Doddington comprises a collection of houses and farms, a quarter of a mile from Hunsterson and about 3 miles from Audlem, right on the southern edge of Cheshire. Even today, the area is completely rural and narrow lanes twist and wind through the countryside, the fields shielded by high banks on each side.

In 1835, Sir John Delves Broughton, of Doddington Hall, owned much of the surrounding land. The Broughton family had been at Doddington for centuries, but when Sir Brian Broughton, 3rd Baronet, married Elizabeth Delves, daughter of Sir Thomas Delves of Doddington in 1748, the two surnames were combined. Sir John, the 7th Baronet, was born in 1769 and married Elizabeth Egerton in 1792.

Under Sir John's management, the estate prospered and was by far the largest employer of labour in the district. In 1835, Mary Malpas, nearly 16 years old, was working as a maid at the house of Sir John's land agent, Henry Davison, where she lived in, although her parents' house was only a mile away. Mary was one of six children, and by all accounts she was an intelligent girl with pleasing manners, although people said of her that she had an address rather superior to her station in life, hinting that she perhaps regarded herself as somewhat above her fellow estate-workers.

On Monday evening, 28 June 1835, Mary retired to bed at about 9.30 p.m. in her usual good spirits, no doubt needing an early night after a hard day's work and knowing that she would have to be up very early the next morning to prepare the family breakfast. Just after midnight, the young girl, fully dressed, knocked on the Davisons' bedroom door in a state of alarm and a rather bleary-eyed Mrs Davison got up to see what was the matter. Mary explained that she had been brought word that her mother was dangerously ill and near to death, and she wanted permission to go home directly to see if there was anything that she could do to help. She did not say who the person was who had brought her this bad news or how he/she had managed to awaken her without disturbing the rest of the household, but in view of Mary's obvious distress Mrs Davison quickly gave her consent and the young girl went downstairs and out into the night.

Mrs Davison followed her down and noted that the front door was locked, presumably from the outside, and the key which was normally left on the sideboard in the parlour was missing. She supposed this had been taken by the distressed girl so that she could let herself in upon her return and so, satisfied that everything was in order, she went back to bed.

The next morning, some time before 6 a.m., the household roused itself for the day's work, and to her alarm Mrs Davison found that both front and back doors were wide open. In addition, a ladder, which had been brought from one of the farm buildings, was discovered on the ground under the window of Mary's room although Mary herself was nowhere to be seen. However, the grim details of her whereabouts were shortly to be disclosed.

At about 5 a.m., cowman Simeon Davis had set out to bring in his master's cattle, aided by Ralph Latham, and passing through Chapel Field, Hunsterson, less than half a mile away from the Davisons', he saw the body of a woman lying against the hedge – it was Mary Malpas. The girl was lying on her back, her head leaning towards her right side, with her skirt and petticoats in disorder, her bonnet torn in front as if during a struggle and her cloak rucked up under her head. A comb and two clean aprons, neatly folded, lay by the body, which was cold to the touch. The dead girl's face was puckered on one side and discoloured, and at first the two men did not recognise her, although they had both known Mary well when she was alive. On closer inspection, there were marks on the girl's neck and the ground where the corpse lay was much disturbed, as though she had struggled against her attacker. Leaving the body as it was, they hurried back to the farm to raise the alarm, meeting several people along the way and telling them of their shocking discovery.

The horrified Davisons immediately sent for the local surgeon, Dr John Twemlow, who arrived at the site at about 10 a.m. He found considerable blackness round the neck and scratches, all of which appeared to have been the result of attempted strangulation. There were also markings and discolouration on the inside of the thighs; however, he did not think that the unfortunate girl had been raped.

Mary's body was taken to Hunsterson Lodge, the home of her parents John and Anne Malpas. Here, another surgeon, Dr Barker, examined the body at about 4 p.m. His evidence at the subsequent inquest disclosed that there had been much pressure and violence on each side of Mary's windpipe, with the appearance of fingernails penetrating through the skin. On making an examination of the lower body, he had found much redness and discolouration about the thighs, produced apparently from excess friction, as though she had been struggling violently with someone. He agreed with his colleague that Mary had been strangled.

Meanwhile, about an hour after the girl's body had been discovered, a labourer, John Shuker, was attending to Mr Davison's cattle and went into the hay crib to collect the calves. To his horror, he discovered the body of

50-year-old Thomas Bagguley, a labourer also in the employ of Mr Davison, hanging from a cord tied tightly round his neck. It appeared that Bagguley had climbed up the loft ladder, put the noose round his neck and, after tying the other end to the top rung of the ladder, thrown himself off.

Leaving the body hanging, Shuker ran for assistance and found the unfortunate Simeon Davis and Ralph Latham, who were still in shock following their earlier discovery. The three men hurried back to the hay crib, where Davis took out a knife and cut the dead man down, laying his body on the floor. Bagguley had a wife and eight children and was known as a quiet, honest and hardworking man not much given to conversation; yet only the day before, he and Shuker had shared a convivial drink at the local inn. According to Shuker's evidence at the inquest, Bagguley had been 'in good spirits and very pleasant, as much so as I ever saw him. I never saw any signs of insanity in him, and had known him for some years.'

Despite this, suspicion was instantly mounted on Bagguley for the murder of Mary Malpas and a coroner's inquest on the dead girl was hastily convened before Mr F. Thomas. A jury was sworn in, with Mr George of Doddington Farm as foreman. It must be noted that in such a small community the jury members would all have been known to one another. Most, if not all, of them would have been employed on the Broughton estate, beholden to Sir John Broughton, through his land agent Davison, and dependent upon him for their livelihood and for the tied cottages that went with it.

The jury set off to view Mary's body at her parents' house, but because of a lack of space there the inquest adjourned to the house of a Mr Dobson. Here, it was stated that the field where the corpse lay had no footpath going through it, neither was it the shortest way to Mary's parents' home. Mrs Davison gave evidence that she had been woken by her maid with the story of her mother's illness, and that she had found the door locked after Mary had left on her journey. The doctors also gave their evidence. Neither was of the opinion that Mary had actually been raped, although it seemed likely that the girl had been killed during the struggle to protect her honour.

John Shuker gave evidence of discovering Thomas Bagguley's body and, after the corpse had been cut down, of finding several keys in the dead man's pocket. These included the key to the Davisons' property which Mary Malpas had taken, the fact of which was confirmed by Mr Davison himself.

After some deliberation, the coroner's jury returned a verdict of wilful murder against Thomas Bagguley Sr for 'having in the night of Sunday 28 June, feloniously and wilfully destroyed the deceased, Mary Malpas, by strangulation'.

The jury then turned their attention to the case of Thomas Bagguley, and John Shuker again described how he had gone into the hay crib and discovered the man hanging from a cord. Quite naturally, he was alarmed and somewhat frightened, but he had steeled himself to look more closely and decided that Bagguley, whom he recognised, was quite dead. When telling how he went out to look for help, he was admonished by one of the jury, who told him that should he ever again find himself in such unfortunate circumstances his first action should be to cut the body down, in case there was still some life left in it!

Shuker told the jury that Bagguley had not turned in for work that morning, despite on the previous evening having agreed to help him to handle the cattle on the morrow. After reporting this to Mrs Davison, he had gone over to the Bagguleys' cottage and had been told by Mrs Bagguley that her husband had gone out the previous evening and had not returned. She had woken at around 2 a.m. and had gone downstairs to discover that her husband had left the house and the front door was locked, with the key having been slipped under it from the outside.

Her son Thomas Jr, a labourer on the railway, said that his mother had repeatedly asked his father to go to bed at about 9.30 p.m. the previous evening, but that he had refused to do so and she had gone to bed alone at 10, leaving husband and son together. The son had then begun the nightly ritual of locking up the house before going to bed himself, and for the next half-hour had heard his mother call repeatedly to his father to come upstairs.

No explanation was given at the inquest as to who it was that had carried the dreadful news to the Bagguley family, but we can be fairly certain that Mr Davison would have deemed it his duty to take charge of things until the parish constable could be called, and that it was he who had sent word as soon as it was practicable to do so.

No post-mortem appears to have been carried out on Bagguley, neither is there any report of scratches to his body, which there surely would have been as Mary struggled desperately against her attacker. To the jury, however, things were now quite clear. Bagguley, under the compulsion of lust and, one or two of them thought, quite possibly satanic influence, had contrived to lure Mary out of the house with his story about her mother being ill (presumably told to her while standing at the top of the ladder found outside her bedroom window), and then having walked a few hundred yards away from the house with the unsuspecting girl had suddenly attacked her, only to find Mary putting up a spirited defence. It was strange that no one in the area had heard any cries in the night air, but perhaps Bagguley had got his hands round her throat quickly and had been able to stifle her screams. Afterwards, stung with remorse, the wretched man had decided to finish himself off.

The verdict recorded by the jury was that the deceased had feloniously destroyed himself by suspending himself to a ladder with a small cord on the morning of 29 June. At midnight on 1 July 1835, Thomas Bagguley was buried in the churchyard of St Chad's, Wybunbury. Strictly speaking, as a suicide death he was not allowed by Church law to be buried in consecrated ground; but many priests ignored this rule, permitting the burial if it was carried out during the hours of darkness in a secluded part of the churchyard and left unmarked.

The dual death was the talk of the surrounding countryside for weeks afterwards and people crowded into the churchyard of St Margaret's, Betley, just a few miles from where the murder had taken place, to view Mary Malpas's gravestone, which was erected by public subscription. Carved upon it were the following words:

THIS STONE
Is erected by Subscription.
To the Memory of
MARY MALPAS
The beloved daughter of
JOHN AND ANNE MALPAS
Who at the early age of 15 Years and 10 Months
Was on the night of June 28 1835
most basely and cruelly murdered
In CHAPEL FIELD, HUNSTERSON
by ***THOMAS BAGGULEY***
an elderly married MAN.
He escaped punishment of
the law, by adding his own
Death to that of his
INNOCENT VICTIM.
Lone was the place and dark the midnight hour,
Which gave sweet **MARY** to the ruffian's power
Stedfast in faith and strong in virtue's might
She fell a martyr on that awful night,
Now safe from sin and harm, She rests secure
Among the blessed who in heart are pure.

Few tombstones can have told such a dreadful story so succinctly. It is quite clear that Mary's family were certain who had killed their daughter and were determined to leave a permanent accusation in stone, for all to see. Yet questions remain to be asked about this mysterious affair; while Mary Malpas's relatives may have been entirely sincere in what they carved on that damning tombstone, all may not have been what it seemed.

The report of the inquest is almost all that we know about this double murder, but some of the evidence presented simply does not ring true. A young servant girl wakes her mistress in what to all intents and purposes is the middle of the night with a request that she be allowed to go to her mother, who is mortally ill. Surely, the first thing Mrs Davison would have wanted to know would have been how the girl came by this information?

Wybunbury churchyard, where Thomas Bagguley was laid to rest at midnight in an unmarked grave. (Author)

And yet, according to Mrs Davison's evidence, she gave the girl permission to go home without making any enquiry whatsoever. Additionally, no mention was ever made of Mr Davison's reaction to all this. It is reasonable to assume that the knocking on the bedroom door that woke his wife would have woken him as well and that he would have been more than a little curious to know what was going on, but he seems to have asked no questions and demanded no answers, either from Mary or his wife.

Evidence was given at the inquest that a ladder lay on the ground under Mary's bedroom window, which suggested that someone had brought it there and climbed it in order to get a message to Mary. However, there is no evidence at all that the ladder was actually used for that purpose. Assuming for the moment that it was Bagguley Sr who had climbed the ladder and tapped on Mary's window sufficiently loudly for her to be awakened, surely her first reaction on seeing a figure at her bedroom window would have been to cry out and then rush to the Davisons' room to give the alarm? Instead, although she did rouse the Davisons, it was with a cock-and-bull story concerning her mother's illness. (Her mother was in fact in good health, and said that she had not sent any message to her daughter.)

Mary Malpas's gravestone at Betley. (Author)

Assuming that Bagguley did manage to get the message to her, it evidently never occurred to the young girl to ask why he was making this unorthodox approach or why he in particular had been asked by her father to bring the message.

So, having permission from her employer, Mary had left the house by the front door to go to her doom, locking the door behind her. The key, which was apparently the one found in Bagguley's clothing when his body was discovered, is the only scrap of evidence to link him with the dead girl. No intimation was given at the inquest as to how many keys there were to the front door and Bagguley certainly had other farm keys on his person when he hanged himself. If, for instance, it could have been shown that there was more than one front door key in existence at the time, all evidence for Bagguley's involvement could have disappeared at a stroke.

According to young Thomas Bagguley, his father was restless on the night of the murder, having refused to retire at his usual time and he had gone out, without explanation, at about 10 p.m. It would have taken his father no more than 15 minutes to walk to the Davisons' farm, a journey he had made many times before at all times of the day and night, so what was he doing for the next two hours before Mary asked permission to go home to her mother and left the house on her last journey? And why did he go to the farm anyway? If he had really lusted after young Mary, there would have been more opportunities as she went about her daily duties than those presented by concocting the ludicrous tale about Mrs Malpas being mortally ill. He could also surely have expected that the girl would be questioned by her employers before being allowed to leave the house, in which case any attack on Mary would probably have resulted in his arrest within hours.

But what if the murderer was not Bagguley Sr, but young Thomas, a much more likely candidate for the affections of the teenaged Mary? Everything so far has depended on the evidence given at the inquest being the truth, the whole truth and nothing but the truth. But what if there was a cover-up?

What if the suicide of Thomas Sr was used as a convenient method of hushing up what really happened on that summer night?

What follows is unsupported by hard evidence, but the author suggests that it is reasonably in line with the known facts. It makes much more sense to suppose that the murderer was *young* Bagguley, who might have arranged a tryst with Mary and suggested to the impressionable young girl that she sneak out of the house after midnight without saying anything to anyone, although this was a risky business that would probably have resulted in her immediate dismissal if she had been found out. This would explain why the mysterious messenger had not made any noise: he was never there, but perhaps waiting some yards from the house for Mary to appear. Once the couple were together, young Thomas's clumsy attempts at lovemaking had upset Mary, who resisted his advances. One thing led to another and, in his frustration, young Thomas had launched a savage attack on the girl, leaving her for dead. He had then fled back home in panic and blurted out to his horrified parents what he had done. It is reasonable to imagine that his father's first instinct would have been to go to the scene and find out if the girl was really dead, first telling his son to stay where he was and say nothing. Finding the girl cold and obviously dead, he had become overtaken with shame and a desire to protect his son from the inevitable consequences of his act; and, searching Mary's clothes, he had found the front door key and pocketed it, before letting himself into the hay crib and hanging himself.

Once Mr Davison learned of the deaths of Mary and old Bagguley, he would have needed to appraise himself of the full facts before going to tell his own employer, Sir John. Let us suppose that the Bagguleys, seeing Davison hurrying towards their cottage, had panicked, thinking that the land agent had somehow learned the truth, and one or other of them had blurted out the true story to their visitor. Davison was now in a considerable quandary. Two deaths on the estate was bad enough, but if news got out that young Bagguley had murdered Mary Malpas, there would be three, as he would surely be condemned to the scaffold. This could well put Davison's own job in jeopardy, as what Sir John would do when he heard the full story did not bear thinking about, and the land agent, now beginning to panic, could well see that some of the blame might fall on his own shoulders.

What to do? Mary and Bagguley Sr were both dead and in no position to contradict anyone, and Mrs Bagguley and her son could be relied upon to say nothing that would direct the hangman's noose towards young Thomas. Why not blame old Bagguley for the crime and concoct a story about his restless evening, his journey to the farmhouse, and his attempt to lure Mary Malpas away from the safety of her employers' home, therefore diverting suspicion onto the father? It would not have taken many minutes for Davison to impress on the distraught Bagguleys that it was either stand by this story or see young Thomas hanged.

In view of her eminent social position as the land agent's wife, no one at the inquest would have questioned Mrs Davison's story, and all it was then necessary for the Bagguleys to do was to agree with her, embellishing the story with the tale of Thomas Sr having been restless and disturbed on the fateful evening.

After all this passage of time, no one will ever know the truth of the matter, but the author suggests that the second scenario is no less believable than the first, and answers most, if not all, of the questions raised by the original story.

Remains of Wybunbury church (St Chad's). (Author)

4
DOUBLE MURDER

Smallwood, 1883

The village of Smallwood, lying on a former turnpike road (now the A50) between Sandbach and Congleton, is even today little more than a scattered collection of houses, and its main claim to fame is that Josiah Wedgwood and his family once lived there. In 1883, 64-year-old Thomas Earlam and his housekeeper, Mary Moran, aged 62, had lived together for many years, although not as man and wife, in a roadside cottage which was badly in need of renovation. The couple were known locally as 'Old Tommy' and 'Old Mary'.

Earlam had been a farmer in a small way but now, growing into old age, he kept his cottage as a lodging-house for itinerant farm labourers and tramps, who found the place convenient as it stood immediately by the roadside on the old coaching route to London and was surrounded by more than a dozen small farms which offered casual work as the seasons went by.

The cottage, which was in a wretched condition, had at one end a tumbledown shed, or stable, next to which there was a small pantry with a narrow window. Behind the pantry was the old man's own room, which he kept locked, and next to that was what he called the 'house place', a low room about 12ft square running the whole width of the cottage, from which a door opened onto the highway. A partition then formed a bedroom, then came the back kitchen, the smallest room of the house, from which another door opened out onto the road. A further rickety structure did service as a washhouse. There was an unstable staircase leading to the squalid upper rooms over the house place, and from time to time the dwelling held anything up to seventeen people at once. It stood on its own, the nearest habitation to the north being about 120yd away, and to the south, 220yd down the road, was the thatched-roofed Bulls Head Inn (which had started out in 1767 as the Red Lion), with a smithy next door.

On 2 February 1883, along the road came a 35-year-old man, calling himself John White, but whose real name was Patrick Carey. Carey was a strongly built man of middling height, known in the area as a professional 'cadger' and tramp. He was wearing a hard felt hat and a blue pilot cloth coat with corduroy trousers; and the hard lines of his face betrayed the type of wandering life that he led. Reaching the cottage, he knocked at the door and

Approximate site of Thomas Earlam's cottage (by trees on the left). (Author)

was admitted by Mary Moran. White had stayed at the cottage for a short time about eighteen months previously, and before that he had spent some time in the workhouse at Arclid, just over a mile to the north. Mary, who was almost blind, blinked a sign of recognition as she showed him in.

He shook hands with Thomas Earlam, who was happy to offer him a room for as long as he wanted it, but White had little or no money. This was hardly surprising as he was not the sort who liked to soil his hands with hard work, especially when he could beg sufficient from passers-by to keep body and soul together. His only possessions were done up in a paisley handkerchief: with odd bits of food, the proceeds of a day's begging.

The other lodgers at the cottage included Isaac Jones, an umbrella-mender; a farm labourer by the name of Edward Sampey; a sewing woman, Mrs Lavinia Sharman; and a man by the name of John Stack, who eked out a living as a rag-and-bone gatherer. Jones, Sampey and the newly arrived White all shared one room. On Thursday 8 February, Sampey went to Sandbach market, putting on what passed as his best clothes for the occasion. 'What a swell you are', White jeered at him. 'You look like a parson.' That night, before going to bed, Sampey carefully took off his clothes and put them into a trunk which he kept under the stairs in the back pantry, carefully covering them with a sheet of newspaper, 'to keep out the dust', as he explained. Locking the trunk, he placed the key underneath it, showing a rather naïve faith in the honesty of his fellow lodgers.

The next morning, 9 February, Sampey was up early and went into the kitchen, where he found Earlam and his housekeeper preparing breakfast. Stack was outside, oiling his cart, and by 9 a.m. the two lodgers had left the cottage, leaving White still in bed. At about 11.45 a.m. a farm labourer called Norbury was passing on his way to work and noticed Earlam spreading some sheets out on the hedge to dry, the product of his morning's work with Mary Moran. Finishing this task, Earlam went inside the cottage and shut the door. Some 20 minutes later, a man named Bracegirdle was passing in his cart and looked over to his left to see John White standing in the middle window. It seemed to Bracegirdle that the other man drew back, as if to escape observation.

At 12.15 p.m., Eugene Gorton, a wheelwright, was passing the cottage when he thought he heard a faint groan. Looking around him, he could not see anything to account for this and, being singularly incurious, carried on his way. At 12.40, James Austin was approaching the cottage when he saw John White coming towards him, carrying a paisley handkerchief bundle. He was also seen a few minutes later, walking towards Congleton, by PC William Booth.

At about 3 p.m., Edward Sampey, having finished his labours for the day, returned to the cottage and, to his surprise, found the door to the living-room not only shut, but fastened. Going further along to the washhouse door, he was horrified to see Thomas Earlam lying on the floor in the doorway between the living-room and the washhouse; and on bending down to examine the old man, he discovered that his landlord was quite dead, lying on his back, with his head turned to the left, his left hand thrown out and his right hand bent over his breast. The old man's skull had been completely beaten in and a pool of blood spread out from under it, across the stone floor. A few feet away lay the body of Mary Moran, who appeared to be in a bad way, having been beaten like her employer but not as badly. She had received a severe fracture of the frontal bone of her skull and she was to linger on for a further week before expiring from her injuries. She had wounds above

The Bulls Head Inn. (Author, permission of Mrs S. Evans)

the eyebrow area, another mark in the centre of her forehead and a third higher on her head – all of these blows had fractured her skull. Nearby was a hammer, belonging to Stack, which he had left in the cottage when he went out to work, and Sampey noticed that the hammer, a heavy one, had fresh blood on it. On a sudden thought, Sampey rushed to the stairs and found to his dismay that his box had been unlocked and the contents, together with a post office savings bank book, were gone. The newspaper which had been protecting them against the dust was now stained with blood.

He ran out of the cottage and along the road towards the Bulls Head, shouting at the top of his voice and soon attracting the attention of passers-by, who followed him back into the cottage, recoiling in horror at what they saw in the washhouse. An old woman, Mrs Platt, was brought in to minister to the grievously wounded Mary Moran.

By now, word was spreading and the cottage was filling with sightseers. A young man named Gorton set off for Sandbach to summon medical help, and James Austin went to find the Smallwood constable. In a while, they were joined by Isaac Jones and John Stack, and a quarter of an hour later Sergeant Oldham and several constables from Sandbach appeared and quickly took charge of the murder scene. There was evidence of great disorder in the cottage, with shoes and clothing lying about as if discarded in great haste. Kneeling over the rapidly cooling body of Thomas Earlam, the sergeant felt in the dead man's pockets, which were completely empty, and it was clear from the looks of Earlam's disarranged clothing that someone had searched the body before him. Going into the washhouse, from where the woman's body had now been moved into the cottage, he saw the hammer, covered in blood, and noted that there were blood splashes right up to ceiling level. A pool of blood spread from under a three-legged table, which also had spots of blood on the top and the legs. In the house, Mary Moran lay unconscious, her clothes soaked in blood and water, and her pockets turned out and empty. There was no trace of John White or his few miserable belongings, and Oldham now set in motion a search for the missing man.

The *Chronicle* of 12 February 1883 headlined the account of the crime 'Double Murder in Cheshire'. It claimed that the murder weapons were a hammer, a crowbar and a billhook and reported that 'not since the murder of "Gentleman Beech" has the neighbourhood been in such a state of excitement'. That murder had taken place seven years before, at Batchton, about 1½ miles from Smallwood, and a newspaper at the time had protested that the Sandbach area was now gaining not only a reputation for murder, but of murders for which the perpetrators remained undiscovered! 'Gentleman Beech' had been dispatched with a hatchet to the head, but neither the reason for the crime nor the guilty party was ever discovered.

The scene of the murder became a huge centre of attention on the following Sunday, with crowds of people from the Potteries, Congleton and Sandbach arriving at the cottage in gigs, traps and any other conveyances they could lay their hands on. The *Chronicle* reported that the village was as crowded as on a fair day and the road to Sandbach had the appearance of a gala, lined with sellers of all manner of food and drink.

In the next two days, the cottage was visited by Superintendent Hindley of Middlewich and the recently appointed Chief Constable of the Cheshire force, Captain (later Colonel) John H. Hamersley, as well as a posse of magistrates eager to take a dying deposition from Mary Moran, who, however, lay still unconscious. A firm of Macclesfield solicitors also sent round a man to measure the dead man for a coffin!

A notice put out by the police stated that the only person unaccounted for was John White, who was now a wanted man and would be charged with the murder of Thomas Earlam as soon as he was apprehended. White was described as being 'Not at all conversible, keeping himself very much to himself, aged about 36, and approximately 5ft 7in in height, who was last seen heading in the direction of Congleton.'

The unconscious Mary Moran was being cared for by Lavinia Sharman at the cottage, while incredibly the body of Thomas Earlam lay in a small closet that had formerly done duty as a bedroom. The police now had a theory that Mary Moran had been struck first, while standing by the door of the back kitchen, and on hearing the noise Earlam had come in to see what was the matter. He had then been struck in the passageway between the kitchen and the front wall. The hammer with which he had been struck had a head that weighed about 1½lb, a single blow from which must have rendered him unconscious immediately. Mary Moran, elderly and half-blind as she was, had put up a struggle, and a bloodstained billhook near her body told its own story.

The inquest on Thomas Earlam was held at the Salamanca Inn, Smallwood, barely 100yd from the Bulls Head, before Coroner Mr H.C. Yates, of Macclesfield. After the jury had been to see the body of the deceased, the coroner announced that he would take the evidence of those witnesses who were in attendance and then adjourn for ten days. John Stack identified the coal hammer, which had a haft around 15in long, as the one which was usually kept in the washhouse, and agreed that he would know White again if he saw him. Edward Sampey said that he had been living at the cottage for three years and that when he had left it at 6.30 on the morning of the murder to look for work, the deceased had been quite well. Evidence as to the wounds on the dead man was given and the inquest was then adjourned for the ten days in order for the police to continue their investigations.

The following afternoon, the body of poor Thomas Earlam was at last buried, but because the time of the funeral had been a closely guarded secret few people were aware of it until the hearse arrived outside the cottage. The coffin was of plain, unpolished oak with black mountings and a plate that merely read,

The now derelict Salamanca Inn, site of the inquest. (Author)

Thomas Earlam.
Died February 9th 1883.
Aged 64 years.

There were no friends or relatives to accompany the hearse, but several of the village women formed a small procession behind it. At the graveside, it was discovered that someone had forgotten to put the ropes in the hearse by which the coffin could be lowered into the ground and the reins were taken from the horses and used for this purpose. After lowering the coffin, one of the undertaker's men had to climb into the grave by means of a ladder to recover the reins.

The next day, Mary Moran recovered consciousness, but she was still in an alarming condition and little hope was being held out for her. In reply to a question as to who had attacked her, she found sufficient strength to say, 'Jack! Jack!', before lapsing back into unconsciousness. The police were certain that she was referring to John White. It had by now been ascertained that the wanted man had a wife and two children at Glossop, but that lady told the police that she had not seen her husband for some years and believed that he was now consorting with another woman. A reward of £100 was promptly posted for information leading to the arrest and conviction of the fugitive.

Soon, the whole of the area was in ferment as it became known that a man had been arrested in Manchester, going under the name of Jack White but whose real name was now known to be Patrick Carey. Meanwhile, the unfortunate Mary Moran had died, so Carey now faced a double charge of murder. Sergeant Oldham journeyed over to Manchester with two other people who had known the prisoner, and they had little trouble in picking him out from a line of nineteen other men, whereupon he was arrested.

Taking the prisoner before the magistrate the following morning, Detective Sergeant Jackson said that acting on information received he had gone to 1 Court, Ashley Lane, Charter Street, Manchester (a common lodging-house), and there had seen the accused, who when questioned gave his name as John Delaney, from Derbyshire. A search of his room disclosed the coat and trousers that Carey had been wearing at the time of the murders, together with the suit of clothes that he had stolen from Sampey's box. These he had asked a local woman to pawn for him, but she had declined.

Superintendent Hindley of the Cheshire Police then appeared and asked for custody of the prisoner, which was granted, and by the end of the day the prisoner was safely lodged at Sandbach police station. The lady with whom Carey had been lodging, Mary Murphy (described as 'a low character'), was also arrested for receiving stolen goods and conveyed to Sandbach at the same time. News of their imminent arrival preceded them, and by the time the train drew into the station there was a crowd of more than 2,000 waiting. Reaching the police station safely, Carey, who was wearing a new suit of clothes that he had bought in Manchester, was charged with the wilful murder of Thomas Earlam and Mary Moran at Smallwood, to which he replied, 'I know nowt about it.' When charged with the theft of Sampey's clothing and post office savings book, he made no reply.

The following day, Tuesday, a crowd of 600 or 700 people gathered in the square outside the police station, hoping to catch a glimpse of the prisoner. The magistrate, Mr G.W. Latham, decided to hold the hearing in the police station itself, in the presence of Chief Constable Hamersley and a number of newspaper reporters. The *Cheshire Chronicle* described the accused as a 'dark looking man, with heavy set features, who kept his eyes fixed on the table in front of him'. In reply to the charge of murder, Carey denied it in a low, faltering voice, and was remanded for a week. The woman who had been arrested with him was allowed bail on her own recognisance.

Carey, who had been moved to Knutsford Gaol for greater safety, appeared again on Thursday before the magistrates, looking 'careworn and troubled', according to the *Chronicle*. The newspaper also commented that 'his looks were not in his favour'. The police now claimed to have a complete chain of evidence against the prisoner, placing him in the cottage at the time the medical evidence revealed that the two victims were killed, and right up to the moment when he was apprehended in Manchester.

At this stage, Carey asked permission to speak to the magistrates and on this being given, requested that all the money found in his possession when

Knutsford Gaol. (Anne Loader)

he was arrested should be sent to his wife, to assist in his defence. However, although he insisted that the money was his and no one else's, the magistrates turned down his request peremptorily.

Edward Sampey testified that he had heard Carey and the umbrella-mender talking on the night before the murders, with Carey saying to the other man, 'It is hard for them to take my shirt for a penny', meaning that Earlam had insisted on Carey's handing over his shirt as surety for one penny lodging-money he owed. He also confirmed that the suit of clothes found in Carey's possession when arrested was his.

Mary Murphy gave evidence that Carey was in possession of funds, saying that he had bought the suit he was now wearing in Manchester for 15*s* 6*d*. She also recounted that when the couple were at the police station, Carey had said to her, 'Do you think they have found that suit of clothes?', to which she had replied, 'Yes. I told them about that last night.' 'Then I'm done', was his reply. Carey immediately protested that what he had actually replied was, 'It doesn't matter.'

At the end of the hearing, Carey again asked that the money found in his possession be sent to his wife for his defence and, somewhat surprisingly, the magistrates, after consultation, agreed to his request. He was thereupon remanded to the next assizes at Chester.

The trial began on 16 April 1883 in front of Mr Justice Hawkins, with Mr Marshall and Mr Eldon Banks appearing for the prosecution and Mr Colt Williams for the defence. Carey was described as being well dressed and not of the appearance usually ascribed to a professional cadger and tramp, although again the *Chronicle* observed that the lines of his face 'betrayed if not outright malevolence, certainly a sour and uncongenial expression'.

Carey faced the ordeal with resignation, and the only time he became agitated was when Mary Murphy gave her damning evidence about his finances. On the second day of the trial, further evidence was given that the accused had bought clothing in Manchester, for which he had paid cash, and had also had his boots repaired. No witnesses were called for the defence, and the summing-up was straightforward. Mr Marshall, for the prosecution, said that the identification of Carey was beyond all doubt and that the presence of Sampey's clothes in his possession in Manchester was proof positive as to his identity. There was evidence that Earlam had money, but where was it? Only a few coppers were found in the cottage, whereas the accused was known to have been spending freely shortly after the old man was killed.

Mr Colt Williams made the best of a bad job by complaining about his difficulties in being the only counsel for the defence and that he had had to take his instructions from the dock. He could do little more than ask the jury to say that the evidence against his client was not sufficiently strong to justify a verdict of guilty to murder.

After a summing-up by the judge, lasting 1¼ hours, the jury retired. After an absence of only 6 minutes, they returned with a guilty verdict. When asked

Knutsford Gaol and personnel. (Anne Loader)

if he had anything to say, Carey replied, 'I am guilty of stealing the clothes, but anything else I am not guilty of. I am quite innocent.'

Mr Justice Hawkins put on the black cap. He told Carey that he had been convicted on the clearest and most conclusive evidence and forthwith sentenced him to death. As the condemned man was taken below to the cells, those in the courtroom heard him burst into tears. There was no appeal and Carey was executed on Tuesday 8 May at 8 p.m. by Marwood, having received the ministrations of the Roman Catholic Church immediately beforehand. His final words were, 'My Jesus, My God, have mercy and compassion on me a poor wretched sinner.' He was the last person to be executed at Chester Castle.

Smallwood remains the small collection of farmsteads and dwelling-houses that it always was, with the A50 running past the site of Earlam's cottage, long demolished. The Bulls Head has lost its thatched roof, but still looks remarkably as it did when Thomas and Emma Woodward ran it in Earlam's day, and provides excellent meals and good beer. The locals say that from time to time there is a chill in the lounge bar as Mary Moran passes by! A few yards further down the road, past the crossroads, stands the now semi-derelict Salamanca Inn where the inquest was held. The only real difference to the area perhaps is the excessive speed demonstrated by the heavy traffic on what was once a quiet, rural toll road.

5
THE MAN OF BANGOR

Rock Ferry, 1886

In the early morning of Saturday 13 February 1886, the police were called to an altercation at 16 Mersey Road, Rock Ferry, Wirral. The house, which was described as 'respectable looking', was rented for £20 per annum by a Captain McIntyre, who had retired from the sea and was currently away working for a shipping firm in Cardiff. His wife stayed on her own in the house, with only her black retriever dog to keep her company.

Their neighbours at the semi-detached no. 14, George Dickinson and his son John, were awoken at about 2 a.m. by a noise coming from the back bedroom next door. It sounded as though people were running about the room and the elder Dickinson was extremely annoyed at this further interruption to his sleep, for in addition to the present noise they had already suffered the sound of a piano being played badly next door late the previous evening. Suddenly there was a crash, followed by shrill screams of 'Murder!' and 'Police!', which prompted George Dickinson to go down into the front street, blowing a police whistle. (Quite why he should have been possessed of such a handy instrument is not recorded, although the proximity of Rock Ferry to the waterfront could well have called for prompt police action on occasion.) Going round to the back of his house, he heard a crash of glass and fancied that he could hear someone muttering to himself in the back bedroom next door. Suddenly, there was another crash of glass, followed by a man's body hurtling through the air from the upper room and landing in the yard, where it lay moaning and groaning. Dickinson's son wasted no time in going for the police, leaving his father to do what he could for the injured man lying on the flagstones. The man was obviously very badly bruised from his fall, but did not otherwise appear to be seriously hurt. In any event, he was sufficiently aware to offer George Dickinson £10 if he would find a cab to take him home. In reply to Dickinson's questions as to where his home was, the man muttered something that he could not hear clearly.

Within a few minutes, Inspector Asbury and Constable Davis appeared and, after noting that the man did not appear to be suffering from life-threatening injuries, looked round for some way to get into the house. Constables Garrett and Dean also appeared and found both front and back doors were locked; but George Dickinson had a ladder sufficiently long enough for Dean to climb through the damaged bedroom window. He found the room in a great state of confusion, the looking-glass and other articles broken and a set of brass fire-tongs smashed to pieces. The gas lamp was lit and, to his surprise, the policeman discovered the body of a woman on the floor, dressed only in a nightgown, and another woman, fully dressed, sitting on the bed. Both women appeared to have been savagely attacked and were covered in blood, the woman on the floor being particularly bruised about the head and body. The woman on the bed was named Elizabeth Platt, who, it turned out, was the sister of the other woman, 26-year-old Jane McIntyre, the wife of Captain McIntyre.

There were quantities of blood on the floor in front of the fireplace and bloodstains on the mantelpiece, the fender and elsewhere in the room. Supposing the man outside to have been connected with the savage attack on the two women, it seemed clear that he had smashed the glass on the dressing-table, torn the venetian blinds to pieces and, in making his escape from the room, had raised the sash window, in which there were no fewer than seven broken panes of glass, before jumping 30ft down to the yard. Examining the apartment hastily, Dean noticed an empty bottle in the kitchen that had contained stout and a whisky bottle with its top removed but still full.

Dean managed to open the back kitchen door to admit his colleagues, who at once had the injured man carried into the kitchen. They were followed by Dr Nickson, who arrived just in time to see Jane McIntyre expire. Both the policemen and the doctor questioned the other woman, but could get no sense out of her. Nickson's forthright opinion was that she was either stupid or drunk, and arrangements were soon made for her and the injured man, who turned out to be Robert Travis, the 45-year-old landlord of the Swan Hotel, Great Sutton, to be taken to the Tranmere Bridewell, where they were charged with the murder of Jane McIntyre and locked up for the remainder of the night. Platt might possibly have been the worse for drink, but she had enough spirit to resist being arrested and tell the police, 'I have done nothing to be arrested for. I am in a private house and know the law as well as you do.' Platt's hat, shawl and boots were given to her for the journey, but she refused to put them on. Among the items found in the apartment were a pair of boots and two coats, all of which were found to be the property of Travis, who was also in possession of £10 16s 5½d, some of which was concealed in his stocking.

At first, in reply to police questions, Travis, now apparently much recovered, gave deliberately evasive answers, including several fictitious names and addresses, but eventually confessed his true identity. He had formerly been an emigration agent in Liverpool but for the past two years had been the landlord of the Swan Hotel, the property of Jane McIntyre's father, who had died some time previously. His only comment when charged with the murder was, 'I never struck the woman with anything. It was not me at all. It was two men and a woman in the house. I have nothing to ask, but I never struck the woman.' Later, he added, 'I am very near dead. I was attacked by some men in that house and had to struggle for my life.' He then turned up his sleeve and said, 'Look where they scratched my arm. I had to jump through a window to get away from them.' Elizabeth Platt made no attempt to conceal her details and the police had now decided that, while not drunk, she definitely appeared to be stupid!

From enquiries made, the police learned that Travis and Elizabeth Platt had been going about together, although this liaison did not meet with the approval of her family because Travis was a widower with two daughters and nearly twenty years older than his girlfriend. The police also learned that the late Jane McIntyre had been fond of the drink and had been treated by Dr Nickson only recently, which was the reason why her sister had been staying there for the past three days. At this stage, Travis and his girlfriend were charged with the murder of Jane McIntyre and detained.

Mr Richard Crispin, Manager of the Wirral Tramway Company, then came forward and told the police that he had known Captain McIntyre and his wife for about two years. He had called at the house at 4 p.m. on Friday 12 February and had seen Elizabeth Platt, who had taken him upstairs to where Mrs McIntyre lay in bed. He had stayed for about half an hour and then left, promising Mrs McIntyre that when he returned he would bring her some apples, of which she was evidently particularly fond. Mrs McIntyre had also mentioned that her sister's fiancé, Travis, would be calling later that evening.

Crispin returned with the apples at about 9 that evening, to find Mrs McIntyre sleeping and Robert Travis sitting in a chair. Elizabeth Platt was also there and invited the two men to come into the drawing-room, where she played the piano for them for some time. (It was presumably her piano-playing that had so annoyed George Dickinson two hours later.) In the course of conversation, Travis told Crispin that he was going to marry Elizabeth in two or three days' time and he had already bought the ring.

According to Crispin, Mrs McIntyre did not awaken during the whole of his second visit and he noticed that she appeared to be flushed in the face, as if she had taken drink, although so far as he could tell there was no drink in the house and none was offered to him. After about an hour, Crispin left the house to catch the 10 p.m. ferry, leaving Travis and Platt alone with Jane McIntyre.

The dead woman's husband had been contacted by the police and arrived home at around noon on the Saturday, having been told of the whole horrific situation. The police were surprised to hear him exclaim that the murder was entirely the doing of Travis and that Elizabeth Platt had nothing to do with it. 'In fact,' McIntyre declared, 'I shall make it my business to obtain a solicitor for this lady.'

The hearing in front of the stipendiary magistrate at Birkenhead Police Court, Mr C.J. Preston, took place on Saturday morning, starting before

Captain McIntyre could get there. The excited spectators noted that both the accused bore wounds. Platt especially had a black eye, which was very swollen, and perhaps for this reason she shielded her face with a handkerchief. Mr T.M. Bleakley, for the prosecution, said that there would be an inquest and a post-mortem of Jane McIntyre later that afternoon.

Inspector Bennett, who had also been summoned to the house on the night of the crime, gave his evidence, which included a statement from Elizabeth Platt to the effect that her sister had been drinking heavily, possibly a bottle of whisky per day, and had been being treated for jaundice by Dr Nickson. Platt's hands had been closely examined by the inspector, and when he had noticed blood round the tips of her fingernails on both hands, she had told him that she had recently suffered a nosebleed after slipping in the street. On the way to the police station with the accused, Travis had turned to Platt and asked, 'Who are the two men who were in the house last night? There were two, were there not?' Platt had replied that she did not know, but, when pressed by Travis, admitted that she knew the names of the men, one of them being Richard Crispin.

At this stage, the accused were remanded in custody until Thursday and the inquest on Jane McIntyre took place later that Saturday afternoon at the Royal Standard Hotel, New Chester Road, before the Borough Coroner Mr H. Churton. The jury were first of all invited to view the body of the deceased that was still lying on the bed at 16 Mersey Road, watched over by the faithful retriever. Once the jury had returned to the Royal Standard, the coroner promptly adjourned the inquest until the following Tuesday, at the Woodside Hotel, Birkenhead.

On the following day (Sunday), Dr Nickson performed a post-mortem and reported that there was a lacerated wound ½in long, which had penetrated the bone about 1in above the left eye, and there were other lacerated wounds to the head, also to the bone. There was some hair adhering to the fingernails and tips. The liver was nearly twice the normal size and death was attributed to concussion of the brain due to external violence, probably caused by some weapon such as a poker or metal tongs.

The adjourned inquest reassembled on the following Tuesday, with the accused couple present. Elizabeth Platt's face was still very swollen and it seemed clear to the jury that she had been involved in a desperate struggle, while Travis, who was still in difficulties with his back after his fall, had to be helped into court by two policemen. Captain McIntyre, the deceased woman's husband, was actually in the hotel at this time, but was not present at the hearing and seems to have been singularly reluctant to show himself. The various witnesses went through their evidence and the coroner then asked Mr Neale, acting for the defence, if his male client would like to make a statement. Neale replied that he would prefer to have a statement from Miss Platt. She told the court that she had received a letter from Captain McIntyre, on the Wednesday before the murder, asking her to visit them.

When she arrived, she had found her sister in bed and a charwoman named Mary Houghton sitting before the fire with her husband. He was promptly sent for a doctor, who said that he would attend on the following morning.

The next day, Travis had appeared with a bottle of whisky and spent some time in the house before going out, returning later on Thursday evening. On Saturday evening, after Crispin had left for the ferry, Platt and Travis had sat talking and she had asked Travis to go because there were no beds made up in the house. Travis had demurred and so she had asked him a second time, at which he had flown into a rage and started to knock her about. Jane McIntyre had shouted to them from her bedroom and reprimanded Travis, after which he had calmed down. Some time later, Platt had fallen asleep when she was awakened by the sound of scuffling. She cried out, 'Jane, Jane, what is the matter?' The gas, which she had lit some time before, was now out and the room was in darkness. Her sister had appeared and fallen down at her feet, and in a short time she had heard the crash of glass as Travis went through the window. That was all she remembered until the police came.

The coroner addressed the jury, pointing out that someone had killed Mrs McIntyre and the only three people in the house at the time of the assault were the dead woman, Travis and Miss Platt. Mr Crispin had left the house at 10 p.m. and there was no other evidence of a fourth person being there at the relevant time. If the jury thought that Elizabeth Platt had in any way encouraged the attack upon her sister by Travis, they must take that into consideration; however, he counselled them that she and the dead woman were sisters and it was against the instincts of any woman to aid or abet a scoundrel in an outrage of this sort on her sister. If they thought that Miss Platt had had no part in the death of her sister, they should find accordingly.

Within quarter of an hour, a verdict of murder against both the accused was given. The *Cheshire Chronicle* reported that arrangements had been made for Travis and Miss Platt to be married on the preceding Tuesday and that the murdered woman and her sister were entitled to a fortune of £11,000 between them.

At a further police hearing at Birkenhead, the pair were formally committed for trial at Chester Assizes, after Travis had made a statement to the court in which he said that on the Friday evening he had stayed in the sitting-room while Elizabeth went into her sister's room and he had heard them talking about their father's money and property. He had then joined them in the bedroom, and the talk had turned to his impending wedding with Elizabeth. Afterwards, they had continued with the piano-playing and dancing until about 1 a.m., when the two women went into the bedroom once more and he had settled down to sleep on the couch. He had been awakened by a great noise in the next room, but as the gas was out he had had great difficulty in getting his bearings. Finding his way to the bedroom, he had felt a blow on his shoulder and screamed out, 'Murder!' and 'Police!' The bedroom door

Chester Castle, site of many trials and executions. (Author's collection)

had then banged to with a tremendous noise and he had felt another blow on the head, which knocked him down. When he had recovered his senses, he had felt in his pocket for his money and secreted some of it in his sock. He could hear a man and a woman talking, and someone had said, 'You *****, I'll kill you.' Travis went on, 'I moved towards the window and then felt several more blows and again called out "Murder!" and "Police!" I then got onto the dressing-table and something fell, I think it was the looking-glass. My hands went through the window and I got entangled in the venetian blind. I got the window open and I think I was on the windowsill for about a minute, all the time there were voices shouting behind me and then I jumped out. That is all I recollect now.'

The trial at Chester began before Mr Justice Hawkins on Wednesday 12 May 1886, with Mr Clement Higgins and the splendidly named Mr E. Honoratus Lloyd appearing for the prosecution; Travis being represented by Mr E. Swetenham QC and Mr F. Marshall; and Platt by Mr Edward Clarke QC, MP, and Mr J. Eldon Bankes. Elizabeth Platt had obviously decided to use some of her inheritance to employ one of the best defenders in the land in the shape of Clarke (later Sir Edward), who had become the liberal MP for Plymouth in 1880. He was fresh from his amazing success in defending Adelaide Bartlett against a charge of murder by chloroform less than a month previously, and his praises were still being sung in the national newspapers. Later, he would appear for Sir William Gordon-Cumming in the Baccarat case and, most famously of all, for Oscar Wilde in his ill-fated libel action against Lord Queensberry. Clarke obviously did not come cheap, but no doubt Elizabeth judged that it would be money well spent.

Whether that was so remained a matter for speculation as Mr Higgins opened for the prosecution and began to outline the events of the evening of 13–14 February. Patiently, he worked his way through the story in his opening remarks until he got to the murder itself. 'Miss Platt', he announced to the court in sonorous tones, 'was found apparently unconscious on the chair, with black eyes and her face covered in blood.' How did the evidence point to the criminality of the woman? The jury would hear that she had gone on the Wednesday for the express purpose of nursing her sister. They would hear that she was on the most friendly terms with her sister, that she was kind to her, that she attended to her and that on that very night she was sitting on a chair in her sister's room looking after her.

The jury might, at this stage, have been slightly puzzled as to the way things were going. This was hardly the speech of a prosecutor, but everything soon became clear as Higgins next invited the jury to consider that the evidence showed that there was no concerted action on Platt's part at all. 'I suggest', he told the jury, 'that the evidence is overwhelmingly against the man.'

The astounded ears of the whole courtroom next heard him say that what he wished to do (subject to his lordship's approval) was to ask them to give a verdict of 'Not Guilty' with regard to the woman. For a few seconds the court was in uproar, before it was quickly silenced by the judge. Elizabeth Platt looked dazed, and quite what Travis was thinking was difficult to comprehend as Higgins went on, 'I will then put the woman in the box and she will tell the court, as far as she can, what happened.' He asserted that the evidence that he would lay before the jury, backed up by Platt's own evidence, would be complete, and the jury would have no difficulty in finding Travis guilty.

The judge having given his consent, the jury were asked to bring in a verdict of 'Not Guilty' against Platt and she left the dock, her expensive counsel Edward Clarke not having uttered a word in her defence. Elizabeth was now free to enter the witness box and give evidence against her former lover; and it is safe to assume that any affection between the two disappeared very quickly once she indicated that she would be prepared to turn Queen's Evidence against him!

She had known Travis for four years, she told the court in a tremulous voice, and she was not engaged to him, although he had given her some rings. She had to agree, however, when cross-examined, that she had once spent three days at Travis's house and that she had received a wedding-ring and a keeper from him. She was then taken through the events of the fatal evening, and Travis's heart must have sunk when it became clear that, having been let off the hook herself, she was determined that he should stay firmly fixed on it. She recounted the unprovoked attack that Travis had made on her in her sister's bedroom and claimed that the blows he had given her had rendered her almost unconscious with a bloody nose. She had then drifted in and out of an uneasy sleep, with the gaslight still on and the fire burning down. She had awoken to find the room in pitch darkness and while struggling to light the gas had felt a heavy blow on her shoulder, which had caused her to sink down in her chair. She remembered the sound of splintering wood, followed by breaking glass and someone falling out of the window. At this time, her sister fell at her feet, after shrieking 'Police!' and 'Murder!'

Platt then announced that in the police court at Birkenhead Travis had said to her, 'I don't know what will become of me, it was the whisky that made me do it.' When examined by Travis's counsel, she replied firmly, 'I stood close beside him. I do not think anyone else in the court could have heard it.' She went on to say that the money her father had left her had not been mentioned either by her or her sister on the night of the murder.

Mr Higgins, in summing up, confessed himself at a loss to know what defence could be set up. If it were to be contended that the two sisters had attacked the defendant, and that he had struck them in self-defence, causing death in one case, it would have to be shown that the prisoner's life had been in danger. If, on the other hand, the defence case was that the two sisters had been fighting, why should the prisoner have jumped through the window, thus putting his own life at risk? The testimony of Miss Platt, supported in almost every particular by uncontradicted circumstances and conduct, and the statements of the prisoner himself tended to prove that Jane McIntyre met her death by the prisoner's hand.

The jury then heard that the defence would call no witnesses, Mr Swetenham contenting himself by complaining that throughout the case counsel for the prosecution had treated the case as one of murder, as if no other verdict were possible. He wound up by saying that he was not, for one moment, going to say that Miss Platt had committed the murder, but that the evidence was as strong against Platt as it was against Travis. The court thereupon adjourned until the following morning, when the judge commenced his summing-up. He said that the defence had alluded to the fact that Elizabeth Platt had known that she was going to be acquitted and called as a witness, but that he, the judge, felt that the woman had not known when she had entered the court that this was to be the case. Swetenham had tried to imply that there had been a quarrel between the two sisters over their father's legacy, but no evidence had been shown of any ill feeling between the sisters on that ground. The whole tenor of the summing-up was against the prisoner, although the judge did attempt some measure of fair play by reminding the jury that if Platt's story were true, it was very strong evidence against the prisoner; and if untrue, it was gross perjury on her part and she ought to be indicted for it.

Before the jury retired, one of their members addressed the judge, saying, 'My Lord, Mr Swetenham, in his opening remarks, said we would be responsible whether the man would live or die – I refuse to accept that responsibility.' The judge assured the man that he was solely responsible for the discharge of the duty which was cast upon him, which was to determine the facts and come to a righteous, honest and conscientious judgement.

Just 45 minutes later, the jury returned with a verdict of 'Guilty', with a strong recommendation to mercy on the grounds of the murder having been a frenzied act, without premeditation. Travis was asked if he had anything to say and remained silent, but when the judge began to address him he broke in with, 'I am innocent.' Donning the black cap, the judge told him that this was 'another illustration of the wretchedness and misery of the terrible evil of drunkenness' and forthwith sentenced him to death, reminding him that a judge had no power to change the sentence prescribed, even if he wished to, but that he would ensure that the recommendation was passed on to the appropriate quarter.

The case caused considerable interest throughout Lancashire and Cheshire, and Travis's solicitor, Mr R.B. Moore, forwarded to the Home Office no fewer than twenty-one memorials signed by upwards of 9,000 people, including 20 county and borough magistrates, 22 clergymen, 24 doctors and 43 solicitors, requesting a reprieve. In addition, with reference to Elizabeth Platt's statement in the dock that Travis had said to her, 'It was the whisky that caused me to do it', affidavits were made by Inspector Parker and Constable Shearwood, who were in charge of the prisoners, that from the time Travis and Platt were taken into custody until they were finally committed for trial, the policemen had taken the greatest precaution to prevent communication of any kind passing between the prisoners; if Travis had even whispered the words to Platt, they must have heard them. Superintendent Clarke also signed an affidavit to the effect that when the prisoners had entered the dock, they were placed in such a position that no conversation between the two would have been possible, either by sign, token or otherwise, without Parker and Shearwood both seeing and hearing. It was also reported in the press, with regard to Platt's denial that she was engaged to be married, that Travis had sent a letter addressed to the Registrar of Marriages at Great Sutton, which was said to be in the handwriting of Elizabeth Platt. In addition, the foreman of the jury wrote to Travis's solicitor, Mr Moore, on 22 May to the effect that he heartily endorsed the petition then being raised and would be glad to sign it; and on the matter of malice aforethought, he and his fellow jurors thought that there was none. In this, the jury foreman was not quite correct. In the same issue of the *Cheshire Chronicle*, 'The view of another juryman' was published, protesting that the prisoner had seemed clearly guilty to the jury and that the judge had commended the verdict and said that the prisoner's guilt was transparent. He further protested that so many learned and educated people had signed the memorials without having attended the trial and knowing anything about it other than what they had read in the papers.

Despite this adverse view, if it had not been clear during the trial it was now being drawn to the attention of the public and the Home Office that

Elizabeth Platt may well have lied on more than one occasion while giving her evidence and that Travis's 'confession', as stated by Platt, was no more than a figment of her imagination. Whatever love she may have felt for the convicted man had clearly evaporated by the time of the trial and she had done everything in her power to see him convicted.

The *Birkenhead News* of Saturday 15 May 1886 took the opposite view. 'Few persons will be inclined to find fault with the verdicts returned in the Rock Ferry case', it trumpeted. 'Though there was no *direct* evidence that Travis committed the dreadful crime with which he was charged, the circumstances point to the conclusion that he was guilty of taking the life of Mrs McIntyre. It is satisfactory to find that the jury recommended him to mercy and there is no doubt the Home Secretary will give to the recommendation that careful consideration which its gravity demands.' Strangely, after this pompous platitude, it continued, 'The evidence tendered, included that of Miss Platt, who was committed for trial on the capital charge along with the condemned man, *although in consequence of the unsatisfactory manner in which she gave her version of the affair, too much reliance cannot be placed on it* [author's italics], points to the conclusion that the crime was the result of a drunken spree. There was evidently no malice aforethought and many people were of the opinion that the prisoner should only have been found guilty of manslaughter.'

It was becoming clear that if Elizabeth Platt had perjured herself, for whatever motive, the case against Robert Travis was very frail indeed; and it was hardly surprising that on 28 May, only a few days before the execution was due to take place, there came a letter from Whitehall, announcing that a reprieve had been granted. The Home Office obviously felt that it could not go the whole hog and quash the verdict altogether, but this was far from being the end of the story because Robert Travis and his case, even if he did not know it at the time, had attracted the attention of some powerful friends.

The trial had received considerable coverage in both local and national press, and the almost unheard-of transposition of Elizabeth Platt from accused to prosecution witness, in the middle of a trial, had attracted much attention. There were those, trained in legal matters, who viewed the whole affair with great suspicion and who determined that more should be done for the unfortunate Travis, who at least was now safe from the hangman's noose, yet faced life imprisonment. These persons included the High Sheriff at the time, the Hon. Tatton Egerton, Sir William Houldsworth MP, Sir Edward Hamley and Mr E. Whitley MP, the senior MP for Liverpool.

These, and many other notables, wrote to the Home Secretary, expressing their reservations about the case, although the judge, Mr Justice Hawkins, said in a letter dated 27 May 1886 that he still considered that the verdict was correct. He was summoned to a meeting with the Master of the Rolls, and the Home Secretary pointed out, 'A strong feeling is entertained by a considerable number of persons that Travis is wholly innocent and that the murder was really committed by Elizabeth Platt.' Late that month, Mr Edward Swetenham MP sent to the Home Secretary a telegram which reported the death of Miss Platt and her death-bed confession to the murder, but this was soon found to be a mistake. On 8 June 1888, Travis was released from Chatham Prison and *Hansard* reported that on 15 June, Mr W. Redmond referred to the Home Secretary a 'statement of Major Barker, Chief Constable of Birkenhead, to the effect that it was known to the police authorities during the investigation before the magistrates, that Travis did not commit the murder and that it was against the judgement of the police authorities that the case was sent to the Assizes!' The Home Secretary dismissed this, saying, 'I have not seen that statement, nor am I aware that it is authentic', and prosecuting counsel Clement Higgins and E. Honoratus Lloyd wrote a letter of protest at this slur on their good name! At about the same time, Edward Swetenham wrote to the Secretary of State that he proposed that a private prosecution against Elizabeth Platt for perjury be instituted at the next assizes, but nothing seems to have become of this proposal.

With Travis now free, attention became focused on a proposal that he should receive compensation for wrongful imprisonment, and the eminent judge Lord Bramwell wrote on 14 June 1888, 'I heartily rejoice at the discharge of Travis . . . I wish that something could be done for him. Perhaps the Treasury could, but that would only be by showing that he should not have been convicted at the time.'

The Secretary of State for the Home Department, Mr Matthews, by now growing thoroughly alarmed at the turn of events, retorted, 'There is no intention to grant this man any compensation. He has not received a free pardon, and it must not be assumed that he was wrongfully convicted. It appeared, on a careful review of all the circumstances, that there was sufficient doubt in the case to make it expedient that his term of imprisonment should be abridged.'

What he might have added was that if reasonable doubt as to his guilt had been shown, Travis should have got the benefit of it at the trial and his 'free pardon' should never have been in doubt.

In the *Standard* of 20 June 1888, 'Justice' wrote, 'Platt distinctly swore that Travis said in the dock at Birkenhead, "If it wasn't for the whisky, I wouldn't have done it." Travis immediately leant over the dock to his solicitor and begged that he would send for the Bridewell keeper who could contradict this, but the solicitor did not do so. Since then, the officers have stated that it was impossible for Travis to have said anything of the kind without their hearing it. But there is another strong point in favour of Travis. There were two medical men sitting in court waiting to be called for the defence, who could prove that the wound on Travis's temple could have been and most probably was inflicted by the fire-tongs that were produced in court. Why

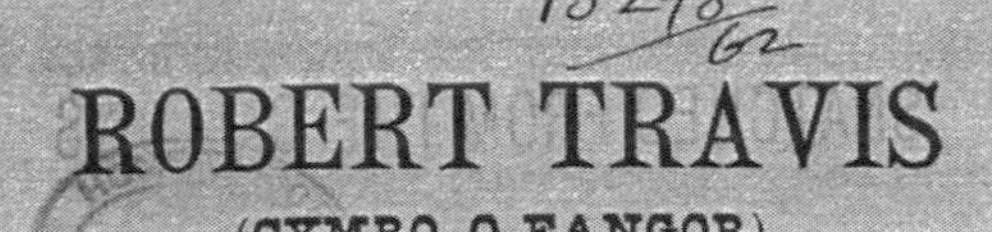

ROBERT TRAVIS

(CYMRO O FANGOR).

SNATCHED FROM THE GALLOWS.

A TERRIBLE EXPERIENCE.

THE SCAFFOLD ERECTED, THE GRAVE DUG, THE COFFIN MADE.

AN HITHERTO

UNPUBLISHED ACCOUNT

OF THE

ROCK FERRY TRAGEDY.

The Trial and Conviction of Travis at Chester Assizes, and his Subsequent

FREE PARDON.

Printed and Published by the North Wales Chronicle Company, Limited, Caxton House, Bangor.

The pamphlet issued by Travis, seeking support. (National Archives)

these witnesses were not called remains a mystery. Travis bore a most excellent character and he has been ruined now and his son-in-law also, through the great expense of his defence and of obtaining a reprieve.' 'Justice' went on to point out that some years previously William Habron had been granted nearly £1,000 when Charles Peace had owned up to a murder for which Habron had originally been sentenced to death. 'Surely', he went on, 'the people of Liverpool will not let the matter rest where it is.'

He might not have been so sure if he had seen the comment in the *Liverpool Echo*, 'The Home Secretary may feel himself justified in refusing compensation from a feeling that if Travis's defence had been better conducted, he would not have been convicted', with which sentiment perhaps one must have some sympathy.

Despite the big guns firing in his support, Travis received nothing from the state and was reduced to printing a small booklet entitled 'Snatched from the Gallows', in which he described events before and after the murder. Printed in Bangor, and published in October 1891, it described the author as Robert Travis, 'Cymro o Fangor' (Welshman from Bangor).

His final appeal read as follows:

> Dear Reader, While I am deeply grateful to many noblemen and ladies and gentlemen for having generously responded to the appeal for subscriptions on my behalf, including the Duke of Westminster, Earl of Haddington, Sir Gilbert Greenall, Bart., Sir Edwin Watkin, Bart., Colonel Cotton, MP for Cheshire, Hon. Alande Tatton Egerton MP etc., the amount realised is insufficient to maintain me very long or to re-establish me in some light sort of business. If there are no others willing to render me pecuniary assistance, may I ask them to do what they can in helping me to extend the sale of this little pamphlet upon which I hope to realise a small amount of profit. When my countrymen once more realise the terrible time through which I have passed, my advanced years and feeble condition of health, pressure may again be brought to bear upon Her Majesty's Government to award me compensation.

Richard Travis waited in vain.

6

'MURDER LANE'

Crewe, 1890

In 1890, 50-year-old Richard Davies had a prosperous tailor and draper's business at 85 Victoria Street, Crewe. A well-built man with a heavy beard, Davies was respected, if not liked, by his fellow citizens and over the past twenty years he had built up a considerable business empire, owning two shops in Victoria Street and another two in Heath Street, besides other residential property. He also ran a bookmaker's business in Manchester, which involved his making visits to that city once or twice a week. Despite his obvious wealth he had a reputation for meanness, but it was rumoured in the town that he often travelled with substantial amounts of cash on his person.

Davies was married and during the week he lived over the shop at no. 85 with some of his numerous children, including Richard Jr, aged 18, and his 16-year-old brother George, while daughter Emily, aged 13, acted as shop assistant and general housekeeper. His wife, Mary, a short, slim woman,

Victoria Street, Crewe, where Richard Davies had his shop. (Author's collection)

usually lived at another of his properties at Hough, 3 miles away, in a house described in a newspaper of the time as a 'sort of hybrid between a large, comfortable cottage and a farm house'. This building stood on the left-hand side of Crewe Lane, the road from Weston to Shavington, and next door to the village hostelry, the White Hart. Her sons Tom, aged 8, and Arthur, who was 6 and the youngest child, kept Mary company.

Young Richard and his brother George regularly slept at Hough, but their father often came home only at weekends. As the burly Davies was prone to assaulting his wife if anything about her conduct displeased him, she probably found their weekday separation a blessing. It appears that this displeasure was easily incurred and the attacks grew so frequent, including on one occasion his pointing a gun at her, that the elder sons began to intervene. John, the eldest, had left the family home some time before, having had words with his father, and he was now living at Hough, near to his mother. Before he had left the house for good, he had threatened his father that if he attempted to assault his mother again he would take it upon himself to provide retribution. In John's absence, it now fell to Richard to protect their mother from father's violence.

Richard and George helped their father in the shop, but often received little in the way of wages other than their board. However, if their father was in a beneficent mood they might receive sixpence for a week's work, and, if they were lucky, they could expect to receive a bonus at Christmas, amounting to 10*s*.

Just after 11 on the evening of Saturday 25 January 1890, Mary Davies was at Hough, talking to her son Richard, when young George rushed into the kitchen and shouted, 'Father has been stopped by two men in Crewe Lane!' George told the startled pair that he and his father had set out from Crewe at about 10.30 p.m. The night was dark with a strong wind blowing and the pony was old and making rather heavy weather of the journey, so they stopped off at a public house along the way. Davies went in for a drink, leaving his young son in charge of the pony and cart. They then proceeded along Gresty Road and into Crewe Lane, and were not far from home when two men jumped out from the shadows and attempted to stop the pony. George hit the pony with his stick to urge it forward, and when this method failed leapt down from the trap to do what he could to repel the attackers. Immediately one of the men jumped into the trap and dealt his father a dreadful blow to the head, which toppled him out onto the ground. George, terrified, was chased up the lane in the direction of his home by one of the two men for almost 400yd before seeing his pursuer stop and then return to where his companion was wrestling with Richard Davies in the muddy roadway. Too frightened to return, George ran to his home, where he poured out his story to his mother and brother. Richard hastily put on his shoes and went out, shouting to George to follow him, and Mrs Davies went for her eldest son John, who soon followed his younger brothers down the lane.

Approximate site of the murder in 'Murder Lane'. (Author)

There in the darkness they found their father lying by the side of the road, his head battered out of recognition. There was a considerable amount of blood around the body and, in addition to the horrendous head wounds, Davies's right thumb had been cut off and two fingers on the same hand broken. He had obviously been subjected to a frenzied attack.

The body was found some 50yd from where George said the attack had first occurred, and the pony was a short distance away quietly grazing, apparently unconcerned by the mayhem that had recently ensued about him. John sent Richard to Shavington for the police in the still-bloodsoaked trap, but when Richard arrived he found the station locked up for the night and had to drive on to Crewe, where he found Inspector Alfred Oldham and Sergeant Harrison at Eddleston Road Police Station. He quickly told them the story of the night's events, and Oldham asked if it was any use bringing a doctor. 'I don't know', was the reply. The policemen assured him that they would set off for Hough immediately on foot. Richard Davies drove on, but instead of heading back home he went to Victoria Street to tell his sister Emily the bad news. 'Father has been killed', he told her brusquely, before setting off back to Hough, overtaking the police on the way. When they got back to the scene of the murder, the policemen lifted Davies's body onto the trap and took it to the house. At about 4 a.m. a police doctor arrived and confirmed that Davies was dead; nothing more could be done but take his body to the mortuary and come back the following day to inspect the scene.

The ground was a great deal trampled on and there were considerable amounts of blood on both sides of the road, indicating that Richard Davies had tried desperately to get away from his attackers. The trap's seat and cushions were covered in blood as were its wheels, and it excited great interest as two of Davies's sons drove it into Crewe to the police station. A heavily bloodstained tree branch was found at the scene of the attack, and footmarks could be seen passing through the hedge and heading in the direction of Crewe's railway station. A further examination of the scene disclosed the deceased's penknife lying in the road.

The body of the murdered man was examined by Drs Travis and Matthews, who found that the injuries to the head had been caused by a sharp instrument, possibly a hatchet or a hammer. According to George, his father had held in the region of £10 in his pocket when they had begun the journey from Crewe; but at the mortuary, however, they found little more than a sixpenny piece. The dead man's watch had been pulled out of his waistcoat pocket, although no attempt seemed to have been made to steal the valuable gold chain that secured it.

During the day, a considerable number of local people visited the crime scene, obscuring forever anything that might have offered a clue to the culprits. The Chief Constable, Colonel Hamersley, arrived with a number of detectives, who tried to interview anyone and everyone who might have had something to offer about the crime.

Mr and Mrs Moses, who had a small market garden at Hough, said that they had driven over the same spot 10 minutes before the attack yet had seen nothing, and the people in the houses nearest were quite sure that they had heard no cries for help. An enterprising newspaper reporter managed to find George Davies and reported that the boy seemed terribly depressed (hardly to be wondered at) and appeared to be thankful that he had escaped the same fate as his father.

The police soon discovered that this was not the first time that Richard Davies had been attacked. Amazingly enough, three years before, the father and his eldest son John had been attacked at almost the same spot and on that occasion John Davies had driven off the attackers with a milking-stool. The coincidence did not go unnoticed in the town, where groups of neighbours stood in the street avidly discussing the case.

Among the theories put forward was that this was a revenge killing, although nobody could quite put their finger on what the revenge was for. An alternative theory was that Davies had had a disagreement with someone, although again no one quite knew who this mysterious person was. It was also rumoured that the murder had been planned by someone who knew the deceased and who knew the neighbourhood intimately. 'The safe keys have gone', whispered one man to another, and the police first of all confirmed this, but later had to admit that the keys had been at 85 Victoria Street all the time.

The police now turned their attention to George Davies, who still appeared to be in a state of shock. He could recall very little, he said. 'The night was dark and once the attack started, I was in fear for my life. One of the attackers was big and the other small and the man who chased me up the lane was wearing dark clothes and a flat-topped stiff hat.' The police opined that because of the considerable amount of blood at the scene, the attackers would also have been heavily stained.

The following day, 28 January, the inquest on Richard Davies opened at the White Hart Inn, next door to Davies's house. The coroner was Dr Churton and the police were represented by Superintendent Jesse Leah, Head of the Nantwich Division of Cheshire Constabulary, and Detective Britten, of Chester. The jury first of all viewed the body, lying next door, which presented a horrifying appearance, with a deep gash over the eyes at great depth together with three cuts on the right side of the forehead, nearly ½in wide.

The coroner announced that this was a case the like of which he had not had to investigate in Cheshire for many a long year, and it was right and proper that the police should have every opportunity to look over the crime. Therefore, he would call no evidence whatsoever at this stage and adjourn the inquest until the following Friday.

Superintendent Leah announced that at present the murder was something of a mystery, but he hoped that now the inquest was adjourned the police enquiries would eventually be successful. Although robbery could have been the motive, as nearly £10 appeared to have been stolen from the dead man's pockets, the robbers had not taken his valuable watch and chain. Perhaps they had missed it in the darkness.

Later that day, Leah questioned the two brothers again. Richard said that he could tell the police nothing other than what his brother George had said, while George repeated his story about driving his father home. The superintendent had inspected the shop in Victoria Street, and noticing some wood chips in the yard he asked Richard what tool they had been cut with. The reply was that a small chopper was used for this purpose, but when on request Richard produced it Leah noticed that it was rusty and appeared not to have been used for some time. Leah called at Hough later that day and said, 'Without doubt, there is another axe besides the one you have shown me.' Richard replied that there had been another chopper but he had not seen it for some time and when he had last seen it, it had had no handle. That night, just before 11, Leah appeared yet again and asked the two sons if they would accompany him to Crewe to search the shop, looking for the missing axe. They agreed to do so, and by the light of a storm lantern they conducted a search but found nothing. Whether the Davies brothers found this searching in the pitch black night an unusual request is not recorded, but any thoughts they may have had on the matter were soon resolved when Leah took them back to Crewe police station and formally charged them with the murder of their father, to which Richard exclaimed, 'Good Heavens!'

On the next day, the police resumed their search at Hough and discovered an axe head buried in a field next to where the murder had taken place, in addition to the haft, which had been broken off.

The *Liverpool Courier* of 29 January, under a headline of 'THE CREWE TRAGEDY – Reported Clues', announced to its readers that the police were now convinced that the motive for the horrific killing was not robbery, nor the work of a tramp, but that the whole of the circumstances pointed strongly to the conclusion that the incident was premeditated and planned and was committed by somebody out of personal malice. A singular piece of information was now also circulating in Crewe, to the effect that Mr Albert Mosley, who managed a grocery business next door to Davies's shop in Victoria Street, had said that on Saturday night, shortly after 9, he had heard a voice in the yard next door, which he judged to be that of Richard Davies Sr, saying, 'Loose me, loose my throat', but as nothing more was heard he had ignored the incident. The *Courier* also reported that passengers on the train from Crewe to Blackburn on Monday night had been startled by the conduct of a powerfully built man who had got on the train at Warrington, carrying a heavy stick and a bundle. He had appeared sober but uneasy, watching his fellow passengers in a suspicious manner and handling the stick in a threatening way. When the train stopped at Blackburn, the man had got out and disappeared. Nothing more was heard of him.

On Thursday 30 January, Richard Davies Sr was buried in the small village of Haslington, 6 miles from Hough. The funeral party was carried in three mourning coaches following the hearse, and the coffin was covered by beautiful floral tributes sent by his widow and family and friends. The cortège left Hough at 2 p.m. in fog and drizzling rain and passed over the exact spot of the assault on its way to the church. Small groups of villagers gathered at the roadside and hats were doffed as the cortège passed by. Mrs Davies was too overcome to attend the funeral, but four of her sons – John, Fred, Tom and Arthur – accompanied the hearse, as well as her daughter Emily and several family friends. Richard and George, now in police custody, were not allowed to attend. Other people followed the procession in their own vehicles and some even walked the whole 6 miles in the rain, facing an equally unpleasant walk back after the service.

On arriving at the Congregational Chapel, Haslington, the hearse was taken to the churchyard, where it was found to everyone's dismay that the prepared grave was too narrow to allow the coffin to be placed in it. Hastily shepherding the mourners into the church, while the gravedigger worked to widen the grave, the Revd A.W. Potts conducted the first portion of the burial service. However, when the funeral party returned to the graveside it was found that the grave was still not wide enough. Before the disbelieving gaze of the mourners, further work on the grave was necessary before the coffin was at long last laid to rest.

On the following day, the *Courier* announced the amazing news that the two sons of the deceased man, Richard and George, had confessed to the murder. Once arrested, it had not taken long for the brothers to work out that they were in a difficult, not to say dangerous, position, and almost together they had asked to see Inspector Oldham.

George made a statement as follows:

> Saturday 25 Jan. Dick got ready to go home (Hough). He went the back way out and when he got into the yard he said, 'George, I want you to get me a box of pistol caps . . . you need not let Emily know what I want you for. About an hour afterwards, I went down to get the caps and when I got to the shop, I stood looking in the window when somebody knocked against me. I looked round and saw Dick standing there. He said, 'Have you got those caps?' and I said 'No.' I then went and got them and we walked up Victoria Street. Dick said to me, 'I tell you that I think that I shall have a go at our old chap tonight', to which I replied, 'Please yourself.' He also said, 'I shall get that little axe out of the yard. You won't see me before I have him. I shall go home and you must come running in about ten minutes after me and say, 'Someone has stopped my father up Crewe Lane.' I did not think he would do it. About half past ten, me and father started from the shop, driving the pony and trap. We stopped at The Barrel at Nantwich Road and father went in for 10 minutes. About quarter to eleven, we started from the top of Mill Street and we went right on to Crewe Lane. We had got about halfway down when Dick hit him with something and father said, 'Oh dear, dear.' Dick hit him again and then father fell out of the trap and the pony went on a bit. I got out and didn't know what to do, then Dick came running down and said there was someone coming so he went across the fields home and I went round by the lane and got home 10 minutes after him, and said that my father had got stopped up Crewe Lane. Dick got his shoes on and went to Maddocks's and told them about it and he then ran up Crewe Lane and found him.

This statement, which roundly put the blame on Richard Davies, was quickly followed by one from Richard himself:

> I hereby confess that me and my brother George made it up to kill father on Saturday 25 January. I left the shop at around eight o'clock, but instead of going home I was to wait in Crewe Lane for father to come and then I was to come out of the hedge and get hold of the horse's head while George, who was riding with him, should jump up and hit him two or three times. I came behind and caught hold of father and

> pulled him out of the trap. Then George got out of the trap and I went home and left him there to wait until father was dead and he was then to come running home and say that father had been stopped by two men. I arrived home at around 11 p.m. and in 10 minutes George came in and told us. I ran and got to him first, but he was on the opposite side of the road to where I had left him. He was quite dead. I took his money out of his pocket and then Jack (John) my elder brother came up.
>
> We did it because he was such a bad father, not to me exactly, but to George and the rest, and a bad husband to mother. They have been very nearly starved sometimes, for he would neither buy them coal for the fire or meat to eat when he was in a bad temper. May the Lord forgive us. We never thought what a crime we were committing and I hope the law will deal mercifully with me and George. We don't deserve it, I know, but let it be for the sake of my mother and little brothers and spare one of us to them. [Note no mention of sister Emily – Author.]

Inspector Oldham asked, 'Are those correct?', to which Richard said, 'Mine is quite true' then turning to George he said, 'His is not true, but lies. I expected, George, that you would tell the truth. You said you would do. You had the axe and struck father first', to which his brother replied, 'What I have written there is quite true. Did you not come to me with the axe head in one hand and the stale in the other and say, "What shall we do now?" You took the pistol and said that if I did not finish him with the axe, you would with the pistol and you struck him by the side of the trap. Did you not say there was somebody coming and I was to come in 10 minutes and say that father had been stopped by two men in Crewe Lane? I did so and you know it. I never struck father at all and never handled the axe.' His brother rejoined, 'You took the axe with you in the trap. Oh, George, you know you did. I took hold of the pony's head and you struck him while he was in the trap.' At this stage, the two brothers started to argue and were parted by the inspector and taken back to their cells.

On Sunday morning, John Davies came to the cells and was allowed to speak to his brother Richard. As John came into the cell, Richard said, 'I hope you will forgive us for what we have done to father.' 'Is it true then?', asked John. 'It is true, I am sorry to say', his brother replied. After a short exchange, Richard Davies was then taken back to his cell and George was produced.

'Well, George, this is a bad job', exclaimed John. 'It is,' replied his brother, 'but I am innocent.'

The brothers appeared at Chester Assizes on Thursday 21 March, and when the doors were opened at 9.30 a.m. there were more than 100 people queuing to get in. By the time Mr Justice Wills entered the courtroom, there was standing-room only. The *Courier* noted that 'the seats reserved for spectators behind the Grand Jury box were filled by a large number of well-dressed ladies and one or two local Dissenting ministers, while about a third of the occupants of the rest of the auditorium were of the fairer sex.'

The prisoners had been brought from Knutsford Gaol on the previous day, Wednesday, and lodged in the cells at Chester Castle for the night, thus causing those who crowded down to the railway station on Thursday morning to be deprived of a view of the accused. In reply to the charge that they did feloniously and wilfully and of their malice aforethought murder Richard Davies, both sons pleaded 'Not Guilty'. Mr A.P. Roberts and Mr D.A.V. Colt Williams appeared for the prosecution, and Mr Glascodine and Mr Malcolm Douglas appeared for Richard and George respectively.

Mr Roberts opened the case by reiterating the known circumstances of the crime and then called Emily Davies to give evidence, which consisted largely of a description of the comings and goings on the night of the murder. She went on to say that her mother received only 13s a week from her husband to run the households in Victoria Street and at Hough and that her father always ate better than the rest of his family. When Mrs Davies came to give her evidence, wearing 'widow's weeds' and a long black veil, she was allowed to sit down by the judge, in view of her distressed state. She agreed that George had come into the house on the night of the murder, about ten minutes after Richard.

In reply to a question from Mr Douglas, 'Was your husband violent?', she wiped her eyes with a small handkerchief and said, 'Yes, very.'

'And has he threatened to shoot you?'

'Yes.'

'How many times has he struck you in the presence of your children?'

'Several times.'

'Has he attempted to set fire to your bed?' (This question caused a commotion in the public gallery, hastily silenced by the judge.)

'Yes.' (Another commotion.)

'Did he use personal violence towards you?'

'Yes.'

'And did your son Richard come down from his bed and save you from your husband's violence?'

'Yes.'

'I believe that you sometimes sent your little children to Sunday school?'

'Yes, I did.'

'Has your husband ever ill-treated you for doing so?'

'He has charged me many times for it.'

It is rather curious that, in her previous evidence at the coroner's inquest, Mrs Davies had told a completely different story, insisting that her husband had been on good terms with both Richard and George and that the family had lived happily together. She had also maintained that she and her husband had had a very happy relationship, something that she was now obviously denying. However, this discrepancy and her possible perjury at the lower court do not seem to have been picked up by the prosecution.

Thus far, the evidence had tended to show that Richard Davies Sr had been a mean-minded bully, who had treated his wife and family with contempt and had been restrained from harming them further only by the intervention of his elder sons. Mrs Davies was questioned closely about the events of 25 January and confirmed that Richard had come home a little before 11, although he usually arrived home between 9 and 10. Evidence of the discovery of the dead man's body was given by John Davies, who described finding the body and the extent of his father's injuries.

Inspector Oldham was called to give evidence of the night of the arrest. At that stage the two statements were read out and Oldham then told the court that the brothers had quarrelled about these, each maintaining that the other was the murderer.

Mr Douglas, on behalf of George, admitted that the crime must have been committed by one or other of the prisoners, but argued that George deserved sympathy on account of his extreme youth. Additionally, he reminded the jury that George had made no admission of any participation in the crime in his own statement.

Mr Glascodine, for Richard, realised that there was little point in trying to maintain that his client had had nothing to do with the murder, since he had already confessed intent, and tried to show that the pattern of wounds on their father's head indicated that he was much more likely to have been struck by George than by Richard; George was much more heavily built than his brother. However, Dr Matthews, producing diagrams during his own evidence, showed that the fatal wounds had all been struck on their father's right side, and as George had been seated on his father's left this line of pleading did not cut much ice. Referring the jury to the evidence of constant cruelty, in particular to their mother over the years, there was sufficient provocation, Glascodine said, for there to be grounds for a verdict of manslaughter.

In his summing up, Mr Justice Wills told the jury that no matter how badly their mother had been treated by their father, this would not support a verdict of manslaughter over murder. He asked the jury to consider whether George Davies was an accidental assenting party to the crime or an active participant. When, as seemed inevitable, the jury found both brothers guilty after only 45 minutes' deliberation, both broke down and were reported as 'wringing their hands and sobbing piteously, giving way to uncontrollable grief'.

The case continued to excite a lot of local interest and a massive petition of more than 50,000 signatures was raised, asking for the death sentence on George Davies to be reduced to life imprisonment, which it soon was because of his youth. No such clemency was shown to 19-year-old Richard, who was hanged on Tuesday 8 April 1890 by James Berry. When the executioner appeared to conduct Davies on his last short journey, he found a pale-faced, trembling man who had just finished writing a letter to his mother – the ink was still wet – protesting his innocence. He had also written to the minister of religion, who had been trying, not completely successfully, to comfort him, saying, 'I never held the axe and did not strike my father.'

During his time in gaol Richard Davies had lost a lot of weight, and to his horror Berry found that he was so thin that the restraining straps would not buckle properly. Thinking quickly, Berry took a blanket from the condemned man's bed and folded it so that it could be stuffed under the terrified Davies's waistcoat; he was then properly pinioned. The fact that the drop should have been recalculated to take into account the extra weight of the blanket was ignored.

Berry conducted his charge across an open yard through the falling rain, and in order that Davies should not be further distressed by the sight of the gallows the executioner placed the white cap over his head before they got to the scaffold. Six members of the press were allowed to be admitted as witnesses to the execution and, for the first time, the rope was not one of Berry's own, but had been supplied by the Home Office under new regulations. Berry was later to claim that he had lost sleep over this execution, believing Davies to have been innocent.

The *Times* of 5 May 1890 announced that effigies of the Crewe Murderers and Executioner Berry had been added to the Chamber of Horrors, and a small paragraph in the *Liverpool Post* of 31 March 1905, headed 'Reminder of a Crewe Tragedy', told of the release of George Davies from Parkhouse Prison, after fifteen years' penal servitude.

Today, the Davies house at Hough and the White Hart Inn, where the inquest was held, are long gone, replaced by a modern bungalow. Crewe Lane itself, now renamed Back Lane, looks much the same as it did in 1890, but to this day some of the older locals refer to it as 'Murder Lane'.

Present-day site of Davies's shop. (Author)

7

THE GORSE HALL MYSTERY

Stalybridge, 1909

Gorse Hall was a rather dour and isolated stone-built property standing in its own grounds, high on the wooded slopes of Hough Hill on the borders of the Borough of Stalybridge and neighbouring Dukinfield. Built in about 1835 by John and Jane Leech, the maternal grandparents of noted storyteller Beatrix Potter, the house itself was in the Dukinfield police division but most of the grounds were in the Stalybridge Borough police area, situated on the northernmost boundary of Cheshire, hard against Lancashire.

Beatrix Potter visited Gorse Hall on several occasions as a child, the last of which was on 2 April 1884, just after her grandmother Jane had died. In her journal, she described the visit with mixed feelings, noting that the

The substantially built Gorse Hall. (Tameside Local Studies & Archives)

hall was not as large as she remembered from her youth. It was perhaps for this reason that the family decided not to live there after Jane Leech died, her husband having predeceased her by some twenty-three years. Gorse Hall remained shuttered and empty until it was occupied, in 1891, by a well-to-do Cheshire businessman, George Harry Storrs, and his wife Mary Margaret, known as Maggie.

Another view, showing the dense shrubbery surrounding the house. (Tameside Local Studies and Archives)

Storrs, who came from a hard-nosed family of local businessmen, having interests in building firms, mills and steamships, was born on 20 April 1860 and entered his father's business as soon as he could escape from his schooling, at the age of 13. George Harry, as he was always known in the family, prospered under his father's tutelage and married Maggie on 11 August 1891, at which time his father bought the near-derelict Gorse Hall as a wedding present for the happy couple. Whether they were so happy when they first toiled up the steep approach drive and visited the dank-smelling building is doubtful, but they set to work and made a home of the property, decorating and furnishing only those rooms that were immediately needed while leaving the rest to be dealt with as time (and money) provided. They did, however, manage to construct an attractive rose garden, which did something to alleviate the rather bleak outlook, and Storrs later lined the driveway with rhododendrons, some of which survive today.

In 1891, Maggie's orphaned niece, Marion Middleton Lindley, came to live with them, to all intents and purposes as their adopted daughter, and they employed a cook and housemaid in addition to a coachman, whose wife helped with the basic household chores. The coachman's job could have been no sinecure, since he virtually took his life in his hands every time he hitched up the horses and drove his master's carriage up and down the steep and slippery drive. In 1903, Storrs took on a new coachman, James Worrall, with whom he eventually became quite friendly. Worrall lived with his wife Sarah above the stables, some yards further down the hill. For the next few years, life passed pleasantly enough and George Harry continued to build up his business interests.

It was just before 10 p.m. on Friday 10 September 1909 that James Worrall, breathless and red-faced, ran down the hill and staggered into the police station at Stalybridge, with the alarming news that shots had been fired up at his master's house. By then, Storrs was an important man in the area and this crisis produced instant action by the local force, whose Chief Constable was Captain John Bates. Formed in 1857, the Stalybridge police had initially a strength of eleven men in total, rising to thirty-five when it finally amalgamated with the Cheshire force in 1947. On this evening in 1909 four constables and a sergeant puffed their way up to Gorse Hall, to find all the inhabitants safe and sound and a broken window in the dining-room the only sign of disorder.

Storrs was sitting there, appearing calm enough, and was able to tell the police that just before supper was due to be served he had seen the dark shape of a man outside the window and had got up to see who it was. He had then heard a man's voice shout, 'Hands up or I'll shoot!', followed by the breaking of a pane of glass, and had seen a hand holding a gun in the window. Taking a bit of a risk, Storrs had pulled down the window blind, effectively obscuring the attacker's view of the inside of the room, but then two shots had rung out in quick succession. Storrs had made as if to dash outside, but his terrified wife, who was in the room with him, had clutched at him and insisted that he stay with her. He had then shouted instructions to the housemaid, who was just as terrified as her mistress, to go to the front door and ring the bell that was used to summon the coachman from his quarters above the stables. Worrall appeared and was promptly ordered to run for assistance.

Meanwhile, word had also been passed to Dukinfield police that assistance might be needed up at the 'Big House', and some of their men arrived to search the outside of the house and the grounds. They found nothing of interest and no sign of any intruder, but waited until the following morning before inspecting the inside of the house with their colleagues from the neighbouring force. They searched especially the dining-room, but to their surprise found no trace of bullets or bullet holes and no signs of illegal entry apart from the broken window.

Leaving to return to their respective police offices, the men from the two forces muttered to one another that there was something fishy going on: although there was no doubt that a window had been broken from outside, there was nothing at all to show that shots had been fired. Perhaps uncharitably, one or two of them wondered whether this was not a 'plot' by Storrs to encourage the police to keep a closer eye on his property.

For some weeks afterwards, the police did keep a watch on Gorse Hall, often posting a man there at night. As there was no telephone installed at the hall Storrs bought a large bell, which he ordered to be mounted on the flat roof and used in an emergency to summon aid. Once this was installed the police watch was reduced, although constables still regularly patrolled the general area.

Nearly seven weeks later, at around midnight on Friday 29 October, the peace of Stalybridge and Dukinfield was shattered by the clamour of the Gorse Hall bell, which could be heard over a range of some 2 miles. Two out-of-breath policemen soon made their appearance and arrived at the front door, looking rather puzzled as there was no evidence of any break-in. Suddenly, Storrs came to the door, watch in hand. Appearing satisfied that the police had arrived, he explained to the red-faced constables, still panting from their exertions up the hill, that he was just 'testing', a statement which did not entirely meet with their approval!

On 1 November 1909 Stalybridge held its local elections, and as the local police force were heavily involved with assisting in the neighbouring wards of Dukinfield and Ashton no one was available to mount guard over Gorse Hall. At about 9.15 p.m., George Storrs, his wife and Marion Lindley were in the dining-room, preparing to have their supper. Storrs was playing patience at a small table and the housemaid, Eliza Cooper, was making the final preparations for the meal. She left the dining-room and walked towards the adjoining kitchen at the same time as the cook, Mary Emily Evans, came up the cellar steps with a jug of milk. As Mary made to go into the kitchen she suddenly saw a man standing in a crouching position against the back kitchen door which led outside to the courtyard. The intruder, who had a moustache, was wearing a dark tweed suit, with a cap pulled down over his eyes and a muffler round his neck.

Thinking for a moment that it was Worrall, the coachman, she paused and was just about to give him a piece of her mind when she realised that it was not Worrall after all. The figure raised a hand, which the startled servant saw was holding a revolver, and said in a low voice, 'Say a word and I shoot!' Acting on instinct, the cook turned on her heel and dashed back again towards the dining-room, almost colliding with Eliza Cooper, who let out a piercing shriek. Reaching the dining-room, Mary Evans screamed, 'There's a man in the house!', and Storrs immediately rushed into the hall and went forward to grapple with the intruder. Storrs was a powerfully built man, around 50 years of age, and the other man appeared to be less than half that and of medium height. By the dim light of the oil lamp burning in the hall, Storrs thought that he could detect the glint of a knife pushed between the intruder's shirt and waistcoat and, as he closed with him, he saw the gun.

Disregarding his own safety, Storrs made a grab for the man's wrist and the two of them struggled and swayed across the hall, knocking a chair over as they did so. Maggie Storrs suddenly appeared, having seized an Irish shillelagh which was hanging on the wall, and attempted to strike her husband's attacker, who in turn thrust the gun towards her gasping, 'I won't shoot!' She also heard the attacker cry out to her husband, 'Now I've got you!' Maggie somehow managed to get the gun free from the attacker's hand, thrusting the shillelagh towards her husband as she did so, and dashing up the hall stairs towards

The steep drive, down which the distraught Marion Lindley rushed headlong on the night of the murder. (Author)

the attic she had the presence of mind to hide the pistol under a carpet. Meanwhile, Marion Lindley, who had seen her aunt running upstairs, made a dash for the front door and out into the night air, where she stumbled down the drive, through the lodge gates and into Albert Square. In the panic, no one appeared to have thought about ringing the alarm bell and the cook and the housemaid had rushed into the courtyard, from where they ran over to the stables to alert Worrall. He, so his wife told the two frightened women, was down in the town having a drink, but before any of them could say more they heard the sound of the bell ringing violently.

Down in Stalybridge, Worrall was in the bar of the Grosvenor Hotel when through the hubbub of conversation he heard the distant clanging. Ever the good servant, he immediately finished his drink and set off for the hall, possibly passing Marion Lindley in the darkness and confusion as he did so. She had reached Oddfellows Hall, a male-only club, where the members, rather than allowing a violation of their rules, quickly escorted her to the Liberal Club across the street, where there was someone who could look after the obviously distraught woman. 'My uncle is being murdered!' she told the members and, led by Harry Heald, who had mistakenly assumed that there was a fire, eight of them immediately accompanied her up the hill towards Gorse Hall, where the bell was still clanging loudly. It had also been heard at Stalybridge police station, from where two constables once more prepared to make the arduous trip up the hill, this time not as enthusiastically as on the previous occasion. 'It's probably Storrs having another practice', panted one constable to his colleague as they toiled upwards.

Reaching the front door and finding it closed, the Liberals split into two parties and examined the outside of the house. A party of four found the back kitchen door wide open and Harry Heald and Richard Ashton led the way in. What they found brought them to a shocked halt. The kitchen was spattered with blood and the body of George Storrs lay on the floor, facing away from them. Quickly they bent down and were relieved to see that Storrs was still alive, though weak. 'Where is Mrs Storrs?' enquired the injured man. Ignoring this for the more important question, Heald asked, 'Who attacked you?' Storrs again repeated his request for news of his wife, but of the attacker there was no sign.

While two of the men ran to open the front door to let in their colleagues, the others attempted to make George Storrs more comfortable and began to wipe the blood from his head. The only sign of a wound they could see was a cut across the bridge of his nose, but the amount of blood on the floor and splashed on the walls told them that Storrs must be badly injured. In fact, he had been stabbed fifteen times, mostly to the chest and back, but these wounds were currently hidden by his clothing.

Meanwhile, Mrs Storrs was still in the attic, pulling frantically on the bell rope and in such a state that it took two men to prise the rope from her shaking hands before taking her to her bedroom and persuading her to lie down. No mention was made of her husband's plight, and the dazed Mrs Storrs did not ask. It was not until nearly 10 p.m. that she felt well enough to get up and come downstairs to the kitchen, where she collapsed on seeing her husband still lying in a welter of gore. Dr Thomas Williams, who lived in nearby Grosvenor Street, had been summoned by someone from the Liberal Club. He arrived soon afterwards, but the injured man was too far gone and died 10 minutes later.

Sketch of the murder scene in the kitchen of Gorse Hall. (Tameside Reporter)

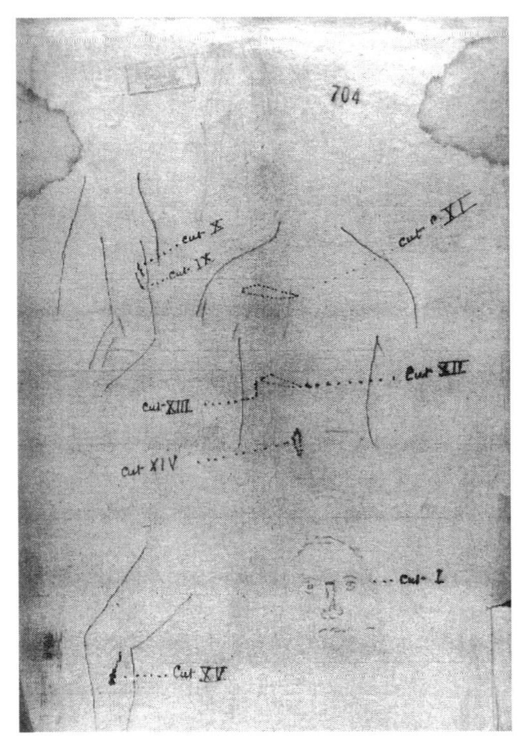

Sketch depicting the wounds to George Harry Storrs's body, drawn by Dr Williams. (Tameside Local Studies and Archives)

Soon, Gorsc Hall was bustling with people. Chief Constable Bates had arrived, followed by Superintendent Croghan from Dukinfield and three constables, plus four policemen from Stalybridge and the eight Liberal Club members. Dr Williams was still examining the wounds on Storrs's body with the assistance of Dr Rodocanachi, whom he had met on his way to the hall. A quick search of the house was ordered, which produced the small revolver from where the dead man's wife had hidden it under the carpet. However, no trace of a knife could be found and it seemed that the attacker had had sufficient presence of mind to take the murder weapon away with him. In addition to the blood on the kitchen floor, there were marks on the scullery door and on the doorknob, and also stains on the scullery floor, on the windowsill and on the wall at the side of the window. The scullery window was broken, ostensibly caused by a tin washbasin, which was found, damaged, outside in the yard. There were also bloodstains on the side of the dining-room door, about 4ft from the floor.

Suddenly there was a commotion outside and two constables appeared, each holding a man whom they had found outside within sight of the house. These two, Matthew Greenwood and Thomas Cottrell, claimed that on hearing the bell they had run up to the house to see what was happening. They had seen a man run out of the house and down the drive, but it had been too dark to identify him. The two were taken to Stalybridge police station for further questioning, but it soon became clear that they had nothing to do with the murder and they were released. Meanwhile, the police extended their search to the town and particularly the railway station, but to no effect, while Mrs Storrs recovered sufficiently to give a formal statement, as did her niece and the two servants.

During the next few days, the police continued with their enquiries and the *Cheshire Courier* noted that the services of bloodhounds had been sought, although with no success. The crime received the fullest treatment in local and national newspapers, the *Daily Telegraph* even going so far as to suggest that the murderer might have been a blackmailer! The inquest on the dead man was opened and almost immediately suspended.

Chief Constable Hamersley appeared, with his deputy William Leah, to take charge of the investigation. A description of the intruder was circulated, but this was only general and would probably have fitted half the young male population of the area:

> About 25 to 27 years of age, 5ft 6in to 5ft 8in high, thin features, very fair to pale, slight moustache.

George Harry Storrs was buried at St Paul's Church, Stalybridge, a few days later amid scenes of great pomp. Crowds of people lined the streets to see the hearse, drawn by two magnificent plumed horses. Nearly twenty coaches of mourners followed the coffin and the blinds of the houses and shops along the way were lowered as a mark of respect. On her return from the funeral, Mrs Storrs announced her intention to sell the house and live elsewhere, the events of the night of 1 November having proved too much for her. In addition, she had a strong feeling that the gloomy stone house was in some way responsible for what had happened, and this somewhat irrational, though understandable, belief was heightened less than a fortnight later, when on Friday 12 November the body of Worrall, the faithful coachman,

Some of the police involved with the investigation. (Tameside Local Studies and Archives)

The substantial funeral of George Harry Storrs. (Tameside Local Studies and Archives)

was found hanging from a beam in the hayloft. The general feeling was that Worrall had blamed himself for having permitted an intruder to enter his master's house, although in truth he could have done nothing to prevent it. The Courier commented, 'It [the suicide] may mean something or nothing.'

The 6in-long nickel-plated revolver left at the hall by the killer had by now been closely examined and found to be of 3.20 calibre, with a ring on the butt. Despite the name 'American Bullock' stamped on it, it was of Belgian origin and appeared to have been tampered with: the swivel pin connecting the hammer and the main spring had been removed; the ramrod was slightly bent; and a cut-down service rifle cartridge had been jammed into one of the five chambers. There was no smell of powder about the weapon, and it did not appear to have been fired for some time.

It is not clear who first mentioned to the police the name of 31-year-old Cornelius Howard, a cousin of the dead man, who had a minor criminal record, mainly for shopbreaking. In 1901 he had joined the Royal Field Artillery and for a time had seemed to settle down, but since leaving the army he had reverted to his old ways. The police were willing to clutch at any straw, and issued a 'Wanted' poster with Howard's description:

> Age 31 years. Height 5ft 9in. Complexion pale, Hair light brown. Clean shaven or light moustache. Slender build and scar on forehead. Pork butcher by trade and fairly well educated. Said to have been dressed,

when last seen in Stalybridge, in a dark blue suit, dark cloth or tweed cap and light lace-up boots.

News quickly came that Howard had been arrested in Oldham, for storebreaking. He had given his name as John Ward, oddly enough the name that the notorious Charles Peace had given when he was arrested for attempted murder in 1878. Howard was found to be badly scratched on the legs, and with bloodstains on his clothing. However, he had a cast-iron alibi for the first Gorse Hall incident, as he had been in Wakefield Gaol on 10 September and had not been released until 7 October. A police line-up was arranged. Mrs Storrs was only able to say that Howard was something like the man, but Marion Lindley had no doubt and picked Howard out of the line of ten men, saying firmly, 'That is the man.'

Mary Evans, the cook, was unsure, but commented that the attacker had a slight moustache, whereas Howard was now clean-shaven. Eliza Cooper agreed with her colleague, although she did concede that Howard looked most like the man, but was taller than the intruder. Howard was promptly charged with murder and appeared before the Dukinfield Magistrates Court, where he was defended by Mr Percy Macbeth and the coloured barrister Mr E.T. Nelson. The Mayor of Dukinfield, Mr W. Underwood, presided.

Prosecuting counsel, Mr Seward Pearce, opened by telling the court that Howard would say that on 1 November, the day of the murder, he was in the Ring O'Bells, Huddersfield, between the hours of 9 and 10 p.m., playing two games of dominoes with the landlord and others for half a gallon of beer. The prosecution, however, would call evidence that these games had taken place on 2 November.

James Storrs, JP, brother of the deceased, said that he had not seen the prisoner for seven years. When asked whether he suspected anyone at all, or if his brother had previously mentioned any names, perhaps of employees he had been compelled to dismiss, James Storrs replied that his brother had mentioned a name, but that it had meant nothing to him. (This presumably meant that the name mentioned by his deceased brother was not that of the man in custody.)

Mary Evans, the cook, was now definite in her identification of the killer, saying that on the night of 1 November Cornelius Howard had been wearing a slight moustache. She fixed her identification chiefly by his eyes, which she thought 'peculiar'.

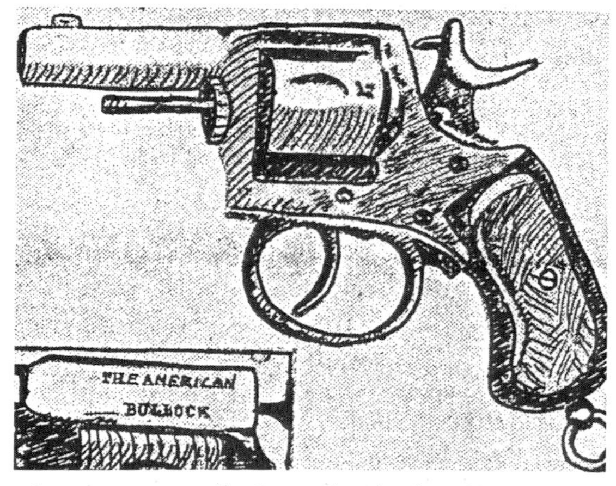

The American Bullock pistol. (Cheshire Constabulary)

Police 'mug shot' of Cornelius Howard. (Cheshire Constabulary)

Ellen Cooper was also definite in her identification of the accused. Next came Maggie Storrs, who immediately broke down and was given smelling-salts by Marion Lindley. She had seen her husband and the attacker in the hall and heard the man say, 'Now I've got you!' The man, who was a stranger to her, had also said that he would not shoot while she had been taking the gun from him. Invited to identify the attacker in court, she stood up and pointed straight at Howard, who was only 2yd from her in the dock. However, she had to agree that at the line-up she had first picked out another man.

Marion Lindley was next to give evidence and pointed straight to Howard when asked if she could see the attacker in court. When questioned by the defence, Miss Lindley protested stoutly that she was not so terrified on the night of the murder that her powers of observation had been affected; and she was quite sure that she could not be mistaken about Howard. She also announced that George Storrs had mentioned the names of two men whom he suspected of the original break-in of 10 September, but neither of them resembled the man she had seen on the night of the murder. The court then adjourned.

On the resumption, Richard Ashworth, one of the men from the Liberal Club, said that he had asked the dying George Storrs if he had any idea of the identity of his attacker, and he had replied in a weak voice, 'No.' However, Harry Heald, another Liberal, contradicted this by saying that he was of the impression that Storrs had been trying to avoid offering a name, and when asked by the prosecution counsel, 'You thought he was evading the question?', simply replied, 'Yes.'

Dr Perk, the police surgeon, described the marks he had found on Howard's person when he was first arrested. There were bruises and a wound on the left side that pointed to a struggle; and he suggested that a punctured wound in the left leg must have been caused by something sharp and could have been caused by the broken glass when Howard was getting through the scullery window at Gorse Hall.

Dr Carter Bell, the Cheshire County Analyst, had examined Howard's clothing and also a large knife found in a pocket. He told the court that there were traces of blood, grease and starch on the knife, which might have been used to cut meat.

Mrs Doolan, boarding house keeper of Joyce's Lodging House, Boardman Street, Oldham, told the court that Howard had slept in her house on 1 November, having arrived at about 11 p.m. She also said that he then had a slight moustache. Barber James Ogden gave evidence that he had shaved off a slight moustache from a man on 2 November, but he could not positively identify Howard as that man.

Howard was then remanded for trial at Chester Assizes in front of Mr Justice Pickford on 3 March, and was represented by the more experienced Trevor Lloyd, with Francis Williams KC appearing for the Crown. Leading the prisoner through his evidence, Lloyd extracted from him the fact that he had cut his leg while breaking into the premises of Messrs Tansey & Walkers in Stalybridge and that he had played dominoes at the Ring O'Bells with several men, including the landlord James Henry Davies, for half a gallon of beer. There was no truth in the contention that he had been at Gorse Hall that evening and anyone who said so was mistaken, Howard said. Later he told the court that although he had seen George Storrs twice in the seven months before the murder, he had not spoken to him, gaining the impression on the second occasion that Storrs was embarrassed at seeing him. Davies confirmed the story about the game, saying that he was quite sure of the date as it had been election day. However, three other witnesses were equally sure that the game had taken place on the following day, 2 November. Further witnesses testified that Howard had been in Huddersfield on the night of the murder and during the following day, and much of the other evidence was a repeat of the previous hearing.

On the afternoon of 5 March, Trevor Lloyd finally began his speech for the defence. 'There was some terrible mystery here,' he told the jury, 'but no possible motive could be discerned, so far as the accused was concerned. Howard's alibi for the night of the murder had not been shaken and his alibi for the other relevant evening was unimpeachable.' He told the jury that the evidence against Howard was weak and he had already demonstrated that it could not possibly have been he who had fired the supposed shot on 10 September. It seemed hardly credible that the two events of September and November were unconnected, so surely being 'Not Guilty' of one also pointed to Howard being 'Not Guilty' of the other?

Francis Williams, for the prosecution, could do little more than point out that Mrs Storrs, Miss Lindley and the two servants had all identified the prisoner in court as the man who had attacked Mr Storrs on the night of the murder.

Summing up, the judge reminded the jury of Howard's prison alibi on 10 September and said that the real issue the jury had to determine was whether the four women witnesses were correct in their identification.

The jury returned in 20 minutes with a verdict of 'Not Guilty', which was followed by an outburst of cheering from the public gallery. This infuriated the judge, who admonished them by saying, 'Now you have ceased that indecent exhibition, I can go on to order that the prisoner be discharged. You ought to be ashamed of yourselves, not knowing how to behave in a Court of Justice.' Cornelius Howard left the court to be greeted by a cheering crowd outside, who promptly accompanied him to the nearest public house to celebrate. The *Manchester Guardian* commented, 'The Storrs murder trial ended as it was bound to do, with the acquittal of the accused man. There was really no case against him.'

No further progress was made by the police for several months. On the evening of Monday 20 June 1910 a young courting couple, James Bolton and Gertrude Booth, were strolling arm-in-arm along Early Bank Road, a lonely lane which ran behind Gorse Hall into Hough Hill Road. At about 10 p.m. they started for home, when they passed a young man who muttered something to them that they could not hear distinctly. Suddenly, the man ran towards them and grabbed Miss Booth round the neck while shouting, 'Do what I want, or I'll cut your throat!'

Artist's sketch of Mark Wilde. (Author's collection)

James Bolton was no coward and leapt to the defence of his girlfriend, managing to free her from the grasp of her attacker while shouting to her, 'For God's sake, run; he has a knife.' In the subsequent scuffle, which lasted for 4 or 5 minutes in Bolton's estimation, he received a knife wound but eventually broke free, and the attacker ran off in the opposite direction. The shaken couple reported the incident to the police at Dukinfield, where Inspector William Brewster immediately linked it with the Gorse Hall mystery.

The attacker was described as being 25 to 30 years old, about 5ft 8in tall and with light hair. It did not take the police long to locate a local man, Mark Wilde, who lived with his parents in Robinson Street, Stalybridge, and had been seen in the district late that evening. A young millworker,

Robinson Street, Stalybridge, where Mark Wilde lived. (Author)

George Hayes, told the police that Wilde looked as though he had been in a fight and had had 'something bright, like steel' up his sleeve.

Wilde was arrested on 23 June at his father's house, 48 Robinson Street, and when charged, replied, 'I have nothing to say.' Later, he made a long statement about his movements on 10 September and 1 November of the previous year. For some reason never fully explained, he had absented himself from the evening shift at work on 10 September, spending most of the evening drinking in the Astley Arms pub opposite his house. As a result of his absence, he had been given the sack. He then claimed that on 1 November he had been involved in a street fight, which had resulted in his getting blood on his clothes. Amazingly, and apparently without prompting, he also confirmed that he had been in possession of two pistols, one marked 'American Bullock', both of which he had since destroyed at his mother's insistence.

At the court hearing on 12 July, Dr W.J. Hancock told how he had examined James Bolton and found that he was suffering from a small puncture wound immediately above the middle of the left collarbone. This could well have been made by the knife now produced to the court, which had been found at Robinson Street.

Both the courting couple and George Hayes identified the prisoner, who admitted in court that he had met Hayes on the evening in question but denied both the confrontation with James Bolton and his girlfriend, and that he had ever seen the knife before. When asked if he had made a statement Wilde said that he had made three, but Inspector Brewster mysteriously said that two of these concerned another matter that the police were investigating. When the judge pressed this, it was explained that the 'matter' related to the Gorse Hall killing, for which the accused was now a suspect. Wilde was convicted of 'unlawful wounding' and was given the very light sentence of two months with hard labour at Knutsford Prison, where he continued to be questioned by the police.

A further identity parade was held on 22 August, but while the two servants now picked out Wilde neither Maggie Storrs nor Marion Lindley could be sure. On 30 August, Wilde was released from his original sentence and promptly rearrested for the murder of George Storrs. On 24 October, Mr Justice Horridge presided at Chester Castle where Wilde, now clean-shaven, was defended by the lawyer Mr Edward T. Nelson, who had also helped to defend Cornelius Howard at his committal hearing. Mr R. Francis Williams QC and Mr Ellis Griffith MP acted for the Crown.

The court was told about the Gorse Hall killing – there was probably no man or woman in the building who had not read and discussed that mystery on several occasions during the past eleven months – and it was explained to the jury that although another man had been tried and found innocent of that murder, there was at the time of the killing a distinct similarity between the freed man and the man now in the dock, although the similarity was not so marked now as then. This observation referred, of course, to the moustache.

Mary Evans, now living in Harrogate with Mrs Storrs, having once pointed to Cornelius Howard as being George Storrs's killer now pointed the same finger at Mark Wilde. She now thought, she said, that Wilde was in some ways more like the man than Howard, although she could not be positive. Ellen Cooper confused everybody by stating that Howard was like the attacker and so was the prisoner in the dock.

Maggie Storrs had a very uncomfortable time in the witness box, Mr Nelson insisting on asking her questions which she plainly found painful. 'Haven't I lived a lifetime since November last?' she asked counsel. 'You forget, Mr Nelson, all that I have gone through.'

Marion Lindley confirmed her identification of Wilde, but admitted that she had been equally positive about Howard.

The court was hushed as the next witness was called, none other than the redoubtable William Henry Wilcox, Senior Analyst to the Home Office, who said that he had examined a jacket and vest belonging to Wilde and had found human blood on them. There was an even greater buzz from the public gallery when Wilcox was given leave to return to London, as he was needed in the trial of Ethel le Neve, Dr Crippen's mistress.

Samuel Charles Wellings, of Liverpool police force, said that he had formerly been in the Worcestershire Regiment and had seen the American

Bullock pistol in Wilde's box while the two of them were returning from military service in Malta, as did Frank Fowles, another soldier in the regiment. Wellings identified the revolver by a series of seven marks on the barrel, the bent cleaning-rod and a ring in the butt.

Mrs Wilde, giving evidence for the prosecution, said that when she was going through her son's pockets she had found a portion of a revolver which had six chambers. No evidence was put forward as to which of the two revolvers this belonged to, if any, although it had already been mentioned in court that the American Bullock had only five.

A Manchester gunsmith, Alfred Pickford, explained that he had examined the American Bullock pistol and had been able to prise loose the cut-down cartridge which had been jammed in the chamber. He had also examined the nose end of a bullet which had been recovered from Wilde's home. The two were more or less identical, he told the court.

There was quite a commotion when the next witness was announced. It was none other than Cornelius Howard, who said that Mrs Storrs had identified him as the man who had been at the hall and that Miss Lindley had told the court that she was in no doubt at all that he was the man. He also agreed to stand in the well of the court with Mark Wilde, so the court could see if there was any resemblance between them. Howard had put on more than two stones in weight since his own trial, so there was now at least a noticeable difference in build.

Finally, Gertrude Booth and James Bolton gave their evidence, which included their identification of the knife.

For the defence, Wilde admitted that he had been in the vicinity of Early Bank Road on the night of the assault but was insistent that he had not seen the courting couple, nor had he ever had a knife in his possession. His friend, Hayes, had noticed his bloodstained clothing, which he had explained by saying he had been in a 'Real Lancashire' fight, which included wrestling, kicking and hitting. The fight was over some imagined slight given to him by a man who was passing by. A former girlfriend, Kate Kenworthy, who had been dismissed from her work by George Harry Storrs (he regarded her as a 'troublemaker'), told the court that she remembered seeing two revolvers on the mantelpiece at Wilde's home.

The jury retired at 4.30 p.m. on 28 October, the fifth day of the trial, and returned with a 'Not Guilty' verdict inside 20 minutes. 'Mark Wilde, you are discharged,' was all that the judge could find to say, other than to tell the jurors that the trial had lasted so long that he would see to it that they did not have to serve again for at least ten years. Wilde left Chester by train and went to Dukinfield, where he enjoyed his 15 minutes of fame in the local public houses.

It seems quite clear that Cornelius Howard had nothing whatsoever to do with the incidents at Gorse Hall. He was in prison at the time of the first one

The site of Gorse Hall today: the house was demolished little more than a year after the murder of George Storrs. The kitchen is the small room, bottom left. (Author)

and it is difficult to believe that he could have invaded the house of his cousin on the night of the murder and not been recognised by George Storrs or his wife.

On the other hand, Mark Wilde had acted strangely on 10 September when he had deliberately absented himself from work. He had no proper alibi for that night and he had certainly been acting strangely on 20 June 1910, when he had attacked the courting couple for no reason at all, while muttering threats that were very like those that were shouted to George Storrs on the night he was killed. Wilde had been in possession of a knife that could well have caused the injuries to Storrs and, bizarrely, had admitted to the police that he had been in possession of the 'American Bullock' pistol, which had had defects in it similar to the gun produced in evidence. It was pointed out in court that all the evidence for the defence came from people who were either close friends or family of Wilde, and it is hard to see why Wilde was not found guilty. The greatest factor against conviction must have been the jury's knowledge that the four women from the Storrs household had already pointed the finger at Cornelius Howard and were just as positive, a few months later, that the murderer was Wilde. Such behaviour in witnesses never goes down well with a jury, and Mark Wilde had every reason to thank his lucky stars. He, like Cornelius Howard, sank into obscurity, and the Gorse Hall mystery remains to puzzle the citizens of Stalybridge and Dukinfield even today.

8

THE JILTED BOYFRIEND

Macclesfield, 1915

Frances Johnson was a bright, steady girl, who worked in the Macclesfield silk trade and seemingly had a good future in front of her. She lived with her parents at 142 Davenport Street, had plenty of friends and until recently had been engaged to her long-term boyfriend, 27-year-old John James Thornley, a lampman on the railway.

Thornley was often to be seen at the Johnsons' house, and his prospective in-laws had been happy enough at the thought of their daughter marrying him. However, about twelve weeks previously something had happened to sour the relationship between the two young people, and on Thursday 16 September Frances was seen by a friend of hers, Lilian Henshaw, in a very distressed state. Her hair was dishevelled, her face was bruised and she had been crying. Lilian naturally asked her friend what had happened, which resulted in further tears, and between her sobs Frances blurted out that she had been attacked by James Thornley. Some minutes later, Lilian encountered Thornley in the street and ran over to him, shouting, 'What have you been doing to Frances?' Thornley replied, 'I don't know', but Lilian persisted and he confessed, 'I have given her a damned good hiding. I feel certain I shall swing for her. I bought her an engagement ring, which cost £2 10*s* and she has pawned it. What man would put up with that?'

There is some reason to suppose that Thornley had been trying to persuade Frances to give him certain 'rights' before the marriage, which she had strongly resisted. Uncertain as to what to do for the best, she had blurted the story out to her father, who promptly forbade Thornley from entering their home again.

In mid-September, the Johnsons decided that they would take a week's holiday, and were evidently quite happy to leave their daughter on her own in the house. Frances, however, did not feel quite so confident and so asked her friend, 17-year-old May Warren, whom she had known for about two years and lived next door at no. 140, if she would sleep over at the house while her parents were away, which she readily agreed to do.

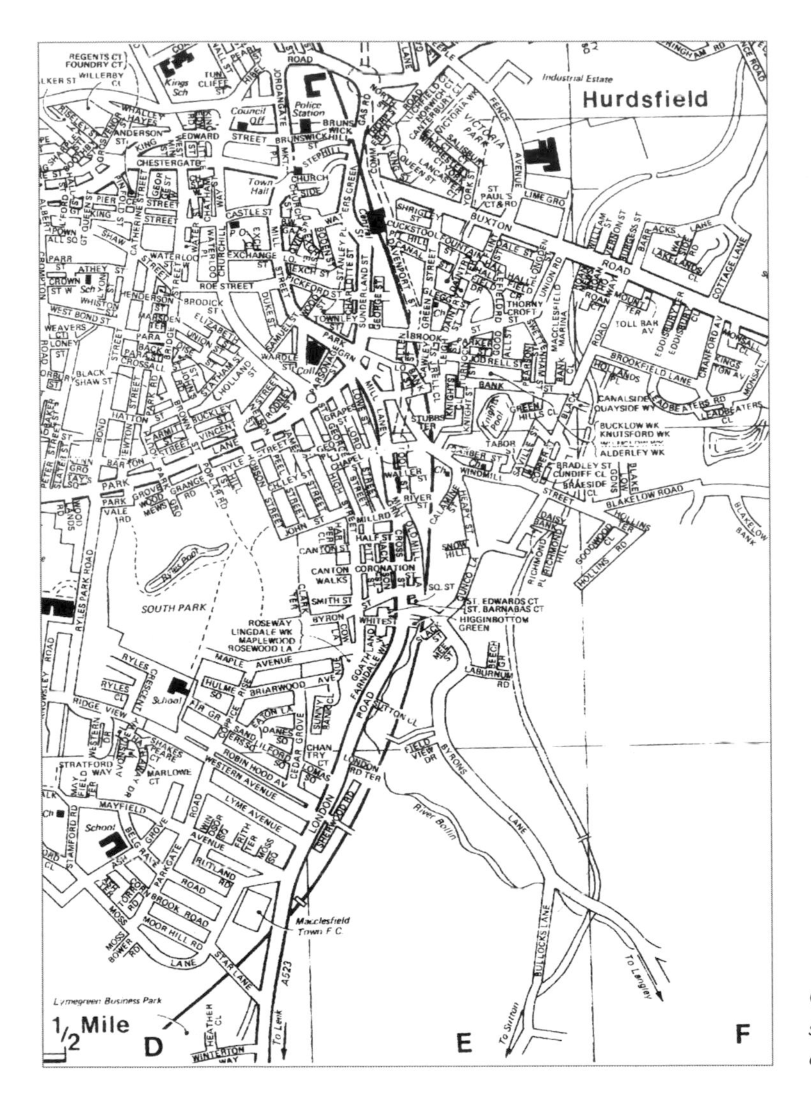

Old map of Macclesfield, showing Davenport Street, top centre. (Author's collection)

On Monday 13 September 1915, the Johnsons left as arranged and at about 8 that same evening the two girls were standing at the front door of the house when they saw John Thornley walking up and down neighbouring Brook Street, although he was too far away from them to speak.

That night and for the next two nights, Frances Johnson and May Warren shared a bed, but, unbeknown to May, James Thornley called at the house during the Thursday and violently attacked his ex-fiancée, pushing her down on the floor while trying to strangle her. Frances fought like a wild-cat, pushing her attacker away, then made for the back door and escaped into the street. May came round as arranged that evening and got the whole story from her friend, who was plainly very distressed. It does not appear to have occurred to either girl to inform a relative or the police.

Brook Street, Macclesfield, where John James Thornley stalked his ex-girlfriend. (Author)

By Friday evening, Frances had recovered sufficiently to suggest to her friend that they should go to the theatre. On the way there, they came across Thornley. He made no attempt to approach them, but followed them into the theatre and they saw him again at 10.30 p.m. when the show closed. May turned to her friend and said, 'Look, there he is, behind us.' Her companion gave the briefest glance and muttered, 'Come along, let's hurry home.' Hastening along Brook Street, they encountered Thornley again – he was clearly following them – and this time, the man spoke to them. 'Good night', he said, but neither girl replied.

When they turned into Davenport Street, Thornley was in front of them and the two girls, now more than a little frightened, hastened to no. 142 and let themselves in, shutting the door firmly behind them. Frances started to prepare the fire for the morning and then went round the house, fastening all the doors. As they were getting ready for bed, she suddenly said, 'May, I want to know if you will go and sleep in the front room?' Apparently without asking why, May agreed, said 'Good night', and went into the front bedroom, leaving her friend on her own. Blowing her candle out, she lay in the darkness and noticed that Frances's own candle had been extinguished before going off to sleep.

At 2.30 a.m., May was awakened by the sound of someone moving about in the house. There was a noise, as though a table was being moved, and then the turning of a door handle, followed by creaking on the stairs. The girl at first cowered down into the bedclothes, then summoning up both her courage and her curiosity she got out of bed and went out onto the landing. In the darkness, she could just make out the form of a man coming up the stairs and the startled girl hastily retreated into her own room, closing the door behind her. Shortly afterwards, she heard Frances calling for help and then say, 'Oh, Father.' Too frightened to go into her friend's room in response to the calls, she stayed where she was and minutes later heard the sound of someone going back down the stairs again. Creeping to her door, she noticed that the gas lamp was on in the kitchen but was too terrified to investigate further. There was now no sound coming from Frances's room and shortly afterwards she heard the clock strike 3.

At about 5 a.m., Joseph Barber, a shoemaker living at 144 Davenport Street, heard May, who was his sister-in-law, screaming, 'Fetch somebody, quick!' Struggling into his trousers, Barber hastened downstairs and into the street where he saw May at the front bedroom window next door. 'What's wrong?', he asked, and was instructed to go round the back where he found that one half of the scullery window had been removed and was leaning against some plant pots in the yard. With May's help, he struggled through and followed her to the back bedroom. 'Frances?' he called three times, but there was no answer. Pushing open the door, he saw the almost naked body of Frances Johnson lying across the bed, covered with blood. There was a bloodstained pillow over her face and in her left hand he could just about make out a shoemaker's knife. Raising the pillow, he saw that the girl's throat had been cut.

Telling the now distraught May Warren not to go inside the bedroom, a command she was more than ready to comply with, Barber hurried off to the police station and then on to Dr Marshall. At 5.50 a.m. PC Plant arrived, and in the bedroom he found the already-stiffening body of Frances Johnson, her throat cut from ear to ear. There were also cuts on the right-hand side of the chin and one on the shoulder. Ten minutes later he was joined by Dr Marshall, who found the body 'quite cold and with rigor mortis very marked'. After further examination, he had the girl's body taken to the mortuary. Here he later performed the post-mortem, which showed that the windpipe and the jugular vein had both been severed. The main wound to the throat was jagged, as though more than one attempt had been made to produce it, and from the centre of the lower edge, running parallel, was another deep wound. On the upper lip, on the right side opposite the eye tooth, was a contused wound, conveying the impression that the lip had been forcibly pressed against the tooth from the outside. A knife was lying loosely in the left hand and there were no signs of cadaveric spasm, which he might have expected to find had the knife been grasped at the moment of death. He was of the opinion that death was caused by loss of blood from the main wounds, which could not have been self-inflicted.

Soon, the news of the horror at no. 142 was all round the neighbourhood and a crowd gathered in Davenport Street, standing silently as various police personnel came and went and house-to-house enquiries were started. Mary Cooper, a laundress from nearby Princess Street, told the police that she had known the deceased girl since childhood and Thornley for about two years, and she knew that he had been keeping company with the girl. Frances Johnson had been in the habit of visiting a Mrs Armitt in Princess Street every morning at breakfast time, and she had often seen Thornley there as well. On the morning of Friday 17 September, at about 7.55, she had seen Thornley go up the entry to Mrs Armitt's house and go in by the back door. Twenty minutes later, she had heard sounds of quarrelling and on entering the house she had seen Thornley and Frances standing there. Thornley had seemed very excited, asking the girl, 'Well, is it yes or no, Frances?', to which the girl had replied in a determined way, 'No! No! No!' Thornley had then said, 'I am fed up with this. I am full up', and left. Frances followed a few minutes later, by which time Thornley had disappeared.

Mary Ann Rowlinson, of Fountain Street, volunteered that she had known Thornley for about five weeks, and that early on the evening of 16 September (Thursday) he had beckoned her into his house and told her that he had been to see Frances and had asked her what she was going to do, to which his former girlfriend had replied that he would have to wait and see. He had continued, 'I went into her house and if I could have locked both doors I would have given her something, but she ran past me into the street, screaming for help, so I gave her about six sharp ones in the street and she will not sleep in that house tonight. She will be frightened. I have been watching her from out of the churchyard.'

By now, the police had enough evidence to place Thornley very firmly in the frame for Frances's death, and on Sunday 19 September Detective Inspector Robinson, together with Chief Constable Henry Sheasby, arrested Thornley and took him to Macclesfield police station. After being cautioned he was charged with the girl's murder, and he responded, 'No I didn't. I want to say that William Mullins, the oatcake man, saw me go home at ten minutes to eleven on Friday night. I got up at five o'clock next morning intending to drown myself, as I had tried twice before, but I couldn't do it. A week Friday, that was. I went to her on Wednesday and asked her what she intended doing, whether she would come back and be alright again and she told me that before she would go with me she would strangle herself, or get married, or go away with someone.'

The inquest opened on Monday 27 September at the Town Hall, in front of Mr H.C. Yates. A large crowd had gathered, but no one was allowed to be present except the jury, the witnesses, the Press representatives and the accused man's relatives. Thornley, dressed in a blue serge suit and wearing a collar and tie, was represented by Mr W. Pimblott and sat quietly, the only sign of nervousness being the way he held his cap, which he twisted round and round in his hands as the witnesses told their stories.

John Hatton, landlord of the Puss-in-Boots Inn, Princess Road, stated that at 4.45 a.m. on Saturday 18 September he had seen a man in the coal yard on the opposite side of the canal, which flowed underneath his window. He had watched the man plunge into the water and swim towards him, pulling himself onto the bank, after which he had walked under the bridge and out of sight.

Hatton had gone out and found a cap, muffler, coat and vest on the footpath, which he had picked up and taken back into the house, then he stood in front of the door to await events. Within a few minutes, the man had returned and

The canal, where Thornley made a futile attempt at suicide. (Author)

stopped close by. 'What's to do?' asked Hatton. 'It's all right,' replied the man, and walked off. When questioned, Hatton identified Thornley and also picked him out of a line of ten men at an identity parade on 21 September.

Hatton subsequently handed the clothing to the police, and in the coat pocket was found a purse, containing 1*s* 2*d*, and several papers, one addressed to 'Mr Joe Thornley, Lampman'. There was also a letter from Beswick, Manchester, which had been posted on 20 May 1915; it was addressed, 'Dear Joe and Frances'.

William Mullins, oatcake-maker, testified that his bakehouse was near Thornley's house and that he usually worked through the night. On the night of Friday 17 September he was at work when Thornley had come in at 10.57. Mullins had asked, 'Where have you been until this time of night?', and Thornley had replied, 'I have been in the theatre and in the chip shop.' Later, around 3 a.m., Thornley reappeared and Mullins noticed that he had changed his clothing and was now wearing a blue spotted muffler instead of a collar and tie. The witness asked, 'Where are you going at this ungodly hour?', to which Thornley replied, 'I have got a bit of extra work to do and I am going to do it.' He then added, 'Will you kindly post this letter for me?', putting the envelope down on the salt box. Going out of the door, he had turned and said, 'Don't forget to post it', before vanishing into the darkness. Mullins had noticed that it was addressed to a Mrs Emily Wigley, 12 Heys Yard, King Edward Street. This letter was later handed to the police.

Another letter produced was to the accused man's mother, which read:

> Mother. Just a few lines. I had a bit of trouble and you will have some more, which I told you. What you said about Frances was not right. When you get this letter you will find me gone and I have left my things to Fenton [Thornley's brother]. I don't want you to have anything to do with them, only to save them for him. Forgive me for what I have done, for I have been brought into it by one thing or another. Don't destroy mine and her pictures for my sake. Bury me in Hurdsfield Church, for God's sake. It is my wish.
> Jack.

A third letter was also read, which was addressed to his brother, in which he told him to draw out money from the bank and also gave directions for the disposal of some furniture. The concluding words of the letter were: 'I am leaving my things to you. Take care of my photo and hers for the sake of me, as I am going away. Tell the old woman I have made away with Frances and give this sixpence to old Granny, from Jack.'

Emily Wigley, widow, of 12 Heys Yard, told the inquest that she had known Thornley for eight or nine months and she had also known the dead girl, as they had worked together. On Friday evening, 17 September, Thornley had gone to her house and handed to her a photograph frame containing a picture of himself. 'Take care of this for me, will you?' he had asked, and she had agreed. He had then said, 'I thought to have gone to the theatre tonight, but that plaguey little thing had gone before me.' 'Well, lad,' replied Mrs Wigley, who knew that there had been some trouble between the two, 'there's plenty of room. You can go and enjoy yourself', to which he replied, 'I will, Ma.' When he left, he had shaken hands with the widow and said, 'I am going to the theatre. If it is ten years to come, I will have my own back.' He had continued, 'I went to Johnson's house last night and gave her what her father daren't do.' 'For God's sake, keep out of trouble,' warned the widow as Thornley went out.

On Saturday morning, Mrs Wigley was summoned to the police station and shown the letter that had been addressed to her. It read:

> Dear Ma, Just a few lines to you, as I went up to see Frances, but she was just in the same mind. So, Ma, if you do not see me before Saturday, pray to God to forgive me what I have done and go to 5, Calamine Street, to my funeral, as I want to be buried at Hurdsfield Church. God help us both and forgive us for what we have done.
> So no more, from your old true friend, Joe.
> P.S. I told you I had done my best. Now I have done my worst. Goodbye and God bless you. xxxxx

After a summing-up from the coroner, during which he told the jury that this was either a case of murder or it was nothing, the jury took only

5 minutes to pronounce a verdict of guilty against John James Thornley. The coroner promptly remanded him to the next Chester Assizes on 25 October.

The trial took place before Lord Coleridge, and the people in the public gallery noted that Thornley's stay in Liverpool Gaol did not seem to have affected him, as he entered the dock in the same clothes that he had worn at the inquest, with his hair neatly brushed. Mr R.B. Bankes KC appeared for the prosecution, while Thornley was defended by Mr Trevor Lloyd. The inquest had already been reported in full by the *Macclesfield Courier & Herald*, whose representative was now busy taking down every word of the trial.

Lord Coleridge started by telling the jury that this was a very ordinary tragedy of jealousy, ending in revenge. The evidence disclosed pretty clearly that the death of the victim was the act of the accused and when that act was once established, it seemed to him that a prima-facie case of murder was made out upon the depositions.

This unpromising start for Thornley continued as Mr Bankes, opening for the prosecution, took the witnesses step by step through the facts of the case. Dr Marshall repeated his previous evidence and, when cross-examined by the defence, said that he had read of persons who, during a fit of insanity, had committed murders, yet who afterwards appeared to be quite sane. He knew that such persons might also appear to be quite normal and rational when subsequently examined by doctors. This attempt to put into the minds of the jury that the accused might not have been in his right mind when the crime was committed was rebutted by Dr East, MD, who said that from 21 September to 8 October he had had Thornley under prolonged personal observation and had been unable to detect any signs of insanity. He was of the opinion that on the date of the murder the accused was well aware of what he was doing. Dr George Griffiths, prison doctor at Liverpool, confirmed this impression, adding that there were also no signs of epilepsy in the prisoner.

Giving evidence for the defence, Mrs Ellen Grant, the accused's sister, told the court that her brother was intemperate in his language, with a hasty temper, and that his grandfather had formerly been in a lunatic asylum. Elizabeth Thornley, his mother, testified that as a child he had suffered from fits and that his sister was also in an asylum. His cousin, Samuel Bradley, had also been in an asylum twice and had twice attempted to commit suicide. Mary Burke, sister to Samuel Bradley, had also been in the asylum for several years – plainly the family were unstable, to say the least. During the past three months, Elizabeth testified, she had noticed a change in her son. He had become more passionate and his food had become consistently unsatisfactory to him. When cross-examined, she said that since infancy her son had been well, but that he had been more passionate since Miss Johnson gave him up.

James Brown, signalman at Hibel Road railway station, said that the prisoner had often exposed himself to danger unnecessarily while at work, and he was of the opinion that Thornley was 'not altogether there'.

That being the end of the defence case, counsel addressed the jury, Mr Lloyd saying that it would be futile to hold out that the crime had not been committed by the accused. Therefore, the question he had to put to the jury was: had Thornley been insane or not when the act was committed? Mr Bankes reminded the jury that Thornley had been in regular and responsible employment for some years and people who had known him had never seen anything to lead them to believe that he was insane. Lord Coleridge's summing-up took an hour, but it took the jury just 15 minutes to return a verdict of guilty. The accused said nothing when the judge donned the black cap and passed sentence of death, speaking in impressive tones and telling him, 'You have been found guilty by your fellow countrymen of the wilful murder of a defenceless girl, determined that if she would not give herself to you, she should give herself to no one else. You were jealous and your jealousy was not only the supreme of selfishness but it was cruel as the grave.' A sardonic smile crept over the face of the condemned man as he left the dock and descended to the cells below.

In mid-November, an appeal was heard before the Lord Chief Justice, which was promptly dismissed. As Knutsford Prison was now being used by the military authorities, the execution was to take place at Walton Gaol, Liverpool, in early December. While in the condemned cell, Thornley told a warder, 'I know Ellis the executioner. I saw him in Manchester once and I expect he'll be the one to do for me.'

The execution took place on Wednesday 1 December. John Ellis, assisted by George Brown, launched John James Thornley into eternity in a double execution, the other condemned man being 28-year-old Young Hill, convicted of the murder of James Crawford on board SS *Antillian*, docked at Liverpool. A seaman named Crockett had been lying ill for a number of days and had asked for water. Hill had offered him some dirty water from a bucket; Crawford had taken exception to this and had begun to quarrel with Hill. Drawing a razor from his pocket, Hill had grabbed Crawford's head and drawn the razor across his throat, and he had died within minutes.

Nothing now remains of the murder scene, Davenport Street having been bulldozed during the construction of the 'Silk Road' (the A523 running from Poynton to Leek). However, Brook Street, down which John Thornley walked, watched by Frances and her friend, still remains, as does the Puss-in-Boots, where Thornley had made a futile attempt to commit suicide.

It seems clear that on the night of the murder, Frances had somehow got word to Thornley that he could let himself in by the back way and come to the back bedroom, hence her request for May to sleep at the front of the house. We shall never know the reason for this, other than perhaps she had begun to feel sorry for her former fiancé, who had never stopped pursuing her since the break-up, but had changed her mind yet again with fatal results when Thornley had arrived and tried to assert his 'rights'.

9

THE PHILANDERER

Wallasey, 1917

Central Park Avenue consists of a row of semi-detached Victorian villas off Liscard Road, Wallasey, at the north-western tip of the Wirral and less than half a mile from the Promenade that runs from the now faded holiday resort of New Brighton to the Birkenhead Docks. The houses are semis in name only, the distance between each pair being little more than 3ft, and each one is built to the same pattern: a glass-panelled front door leading into a vestibule, and from there into a hall, from which access can be gained to the front and back parlours, plus kitchen, with stairs in the hall leading to three bedrooms upstairs. Each house also had a tiny front garden, bounded by a low brick wall with heavy stone pillars carrying a metal garden gate. Inside the garden wall of no. 16, a small privet hedge and a rather desultory little tree struggled for existence in the grimy atmosphere. A lean-to scullery at the back, no more than 10ft by 6ft, completed the accommodation. In 1917, a small back garden at the rear of the house contained a vegetable patch, coals and WC, and in the front street a gas-lamp shed its wavering light on the property at night.

William Thomas Hodgson, generally known as Tom, lived at no. 16 with his wife Margaret and their two children, 3-year-old Margaret (known as Nettie) and Cyril, who was just 1. Hodgson worked as a silk buyer in the old established firm of Robb Brothers, whose premises, together with a lodging-house for unmarried employees known as Sutton House, were situated at Oliver Street, a little less than 2 miles south, as the crow flies, from Central Park Avenue.

Hodgson was 34, always well turned out, with dark hair parted down the centre and a small moustache. He was popular enough with his workmates – according to the *Liverpool Courier*, he was a man with a rather open manner who made many friends. His conduct at the dinner table was said to have been jovial and pleasant, and he was very much liked by his colleagues. It was his usual practice to have a drink at lunchtime with a warehouseman at Robb Brothers, William Marshall Wilson, and the two of them would often call into the Charing Cross Hotel on the way home in the evening for more.

Hodgson and his wife Margaret had been married for about seven years, more or less happily, although Margaret was prone to complain to

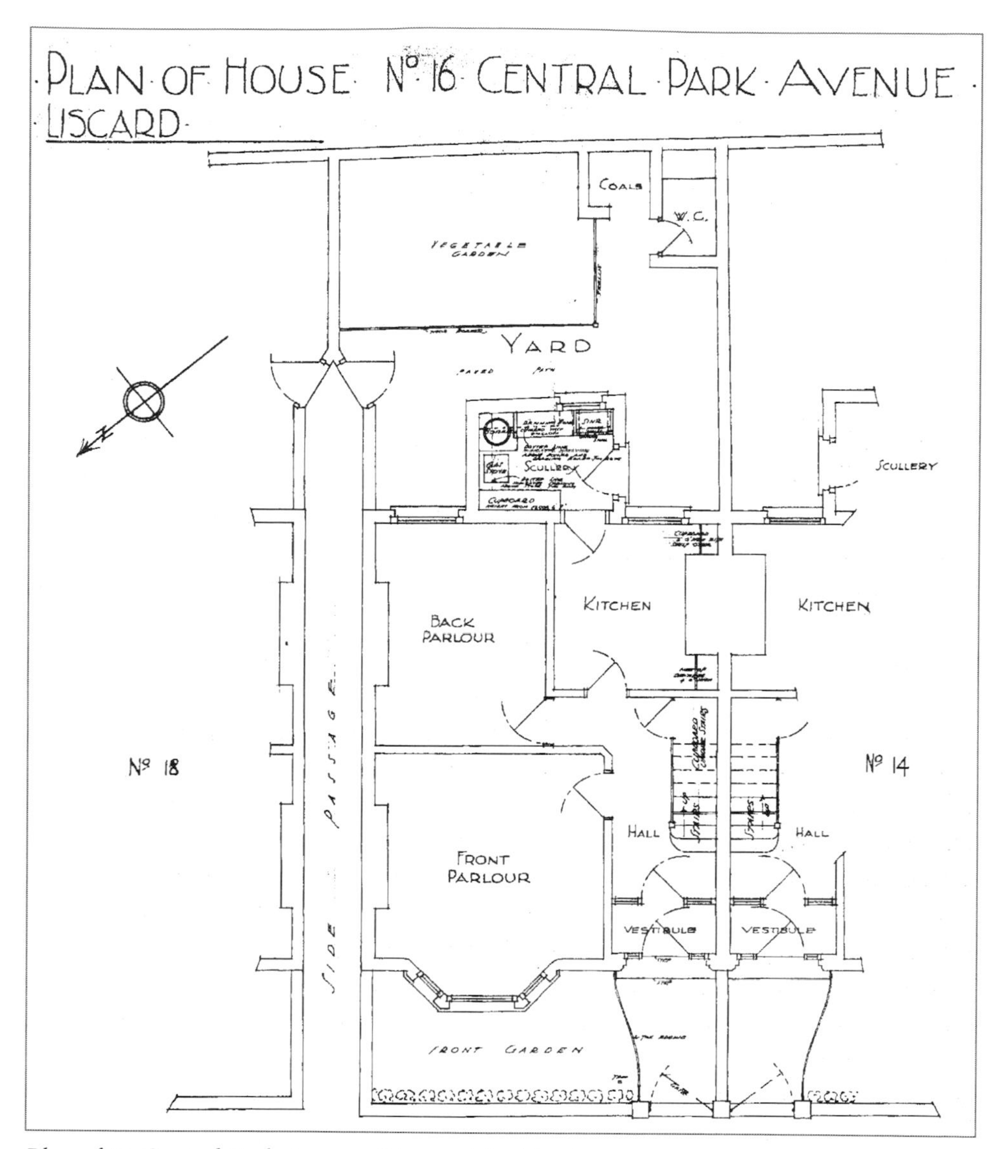

Plan of 16 Central Park Avenue. (National Archives)

her husband about his late-comings, usually after he had been drinking. Hodgson's only defence to this charge was that Wednesday was his night out. According to his mother-in-law, Mrs Mary Ellen Smith, Hodgson had a shocking temper and the family always tried very hard not to 'vex' him. The couple had been courting for about two years before Hodgson persuaded Mrs Smith to let him lodge with them, and he had lived there for another two years before the marriage so they had had plenty of time to see what sort of a man was marrying into the family. The week before Good Friday 1917, Mr and Mrs Smith had stayed with the Hodgsons and thought that they got

16 Central Park Avenue, Wallasey. (National Archives)

on 'comfortable'; but that when Hodgson came home late, 'They would barge on one another.'

The Hodgsons had been living at no. 16 since September 1916, paying rent of around £35 a year, and they got on well enough with Mr and Mrs Law, their neighbours at no. 14, the other part of the semi. William James Law was a post office clerk and his wife Eleanor saw Mrs Hodgson almost every day, although she rarely saw Hodgson himself. On the morning of Monday 16 April 1917, Mrs Shaw came downstairs at about 7.40, and a little later on she heard a child's voice saying, 'Don't do that.' She recognised the voice as that of Nettie, thinking nothing more of it, and subsequently, at about 8.35, she heard next door's vestibule door slam shut.

At about 6 p.m. that evening, Mrs Law was showing a guest out of the house and knocked at the glass panel of the front door of no. 16, which she could easily do by leaning over the low wall which divided the two front paths. She noticed that the front door was open, and on receiving no answer walked into the pathway of no. 16 and opened the vestibule door, knocking on the hatstand in the hall as was her custom. Again there was no reply, although she could hear baby Cyril crying upstairs. Walking into the kitchen, she saw that the fire was out; the table to her left, covered with a white cloth, still had the remains of a breakfast meal on it, including a small white eggcup and plate; and a child's tin money box lay on the table, together with a woman's purse. Glancing round, she looked towards the scullery and to her horror saw the body of a woman, with the legs and feet protruding into the kitchen.

Thoroughly alarmed, she made no attempt to examine the body but rushed outside, almost into the arms of William Samuel Wells, a bricklayer and chimney sweep who was passing at the time. In response to Mrs Law's hysterical request he went into the scullery, and what he saw almost made him turn and run out into the street again. The bodies of a woman and a small girl lay on the floor, almost touching one another. Under the woman's head and to the right of it there was a large pool of blood and a considerable quantity of brain substance, while the head itself was covered in blood and showed several injuries. There was a similar pool of blood surrounding the head of the child and a bloodstained hatchet lay on the floor, to the right of the woman's body.

Cyril was still crying upstairs and Wells brought him down. He handed the child to a neighbour, Mrs Barrow, of three doors away, who found him thoroughly soaked and in need of food. The police were called and Constables Marsh and Barnaby were dispatched from the Central Police Station, arriving at no. 16 at 6.10 p.m. They quickly examined the house but made no attempt to move the bodies, which were both fully dressed. Mrs Hodgson's hair was in curling-pins and the child's in curling-papers, which indicated that they had obviously had time to complete their toilet that morning before being subjected to a savage attack. There were splashes of blood as high as 6ft 9in up the walls and a second hatchet lay under the sink, with bloodstains on the handle. Upstairs, a single bed in the small front bedroom appeared to have been slept in, and in the back bedroom was a double bed, also slept in, and a child's cot, the bedclothes on which were soaking wet. A diamond ring was found on a mantelshelf in the kitchen, plus one single shilling.

Chief Inspector John Morris and Inspector John Bebbington arrived shortly after Detective Inspector Robert John Pearson; and the small house became even more crowded when Chief Constable Percy Linnell Barry arrived at 6.45 p.m. He was accompanied by Police Surgeon Dr Thomas Napier, who examined the bodies and pronounced them dead. Napier was of the opinion that the attack must have been completely unexpected when it came, and that death had occurred some eight to ten hours earlier.

Amid all the hustle and bustle, with a large crowd of people being held back from invading the house by two constables outside, it was hardly surprising that at about 7.15 p.m., William Hodgson was able to make his way home unrecognised and walked down the pathway of no. 14, where the door was opened to him by Mrs Law. He seemed to her to be quite calm, but puzzled at all the activity in the street outside. She quickly told him as much as she knew about the horrible circumstances next door, and some minutes later Inspector

Inside no. 16. Note child's money box on table. (National Archives)

Bebbington, who was attending to the covering of the bodies on stretchers, was surprised to see a man standing just inside the kitchen door. 'What is your business?' he asked curtly. The man replied, 'What's up here?' Bebbington asked, 'Are you the tenant of this house?', to which the man replied, 'I am Mr Hodgson.' Chief Inspector Morris, who was also present, then said, 'Don't be excited. There is certainly something wrong here. Come this way.' Leading Hodgson into the hall, Morris pointed to a portmanteau lying open on the floor, containing clothing and some cutlery, and said coolly, 'It looks as though there is something wrong, does it not?'

Morris continued, 'From enquiries made, we have been unable to find anyone that has been in the house since you left this morning. Have you any objection to taking your coat off and letting me have a look at your shirt sleeves?' 'Not in the least', replied Hodgson. 'Did you change your shirt yesterday?' 'No, I have worn it for a week', was the reply. Morris then took the man into the scullery and pointed to the hatchet. 'That isn't mine', said Hodgson; then, pointing to the small hatchet under the sink, 'That one is mine.'

The inspector then took Hodgson, who was now sobbing, into the back sitting-room, where he sat head in hands until he was taken down to the Central Police Station and questioned by the chief constable, while his answers were taken down in shorthand by DC Keith. On being asked how much money he had in his possession, Hodgson turned out his pockets to reveal £15 in notes, plus two postal orders for 11*s* 6*d* and 2*s* which he said had been sent for his little boy's birthday. A subsequent search of the house revealed a bankbook of the Liverpool Savings Bank and three War Bonds.

A statement was then taken, produced in court as *Exhibit* 21a. This was obviously the result of a long series of questions and answers, and read as follows (some extracts have been excluded where the relevance is not important):

> WILLIAM THOMAS HODGSON states:- I am a buyer in the employ of Messrs Robb Brothers, Drapers, Birkenhead, and reside at 16, Central Park Avenue, Liscard. The deceased is my wife and we were married in September 1910. She was 37 years of age on 2 April last. The little girl, Margaret, now deceased, is my daughter and she was born on 27 April 1913. I have also a boy, named Cyril, and he was 12 months old on April 13 last.
>
> I went to bed last night about 10 o'clock and got up again at 7 o'clock this morning. My wife remained in bed and I took her up a cup of tea at about 7.30 a.m. I had my breakfast in the middle kitchen. My wife got up after she had had the tea. She did not breakfast with me . . . When I left the house at about 8.30 a.m., the little girl was in the kitchen along with her mother. I had previously arranged with my wife that she and the little girl would go to the pictures that night and that I would stay at home with the little boy. The fire was lit when I left the house. I walked

across the docks. I was engaged at Birkenhead until 6 o'clock at night. I do not go home for dinner, but have my dinner on the works premises. I left Birkenhead about 6.15 p.m., the usual time. I had no intimation then of what had happened . . .

I have only one hatchet and I usually keep it at the back. I keep the chopper under the slopstone. I went out by the front door to work. Previously that morning I went out by the back door for coals, but did not lock it again. The money box would be on the mantelpiece in the kitchen containing about 16*s* in silver and copper, small and large and one or two 2*s* pieces. My wife had about £4 in notes and some silver in her purse. She was reckoning up her money last night and I knew she had four one pound notes, one 10*s* note and some silver. She gave me the 10s note this morning. I gave her £2 15*s* on Friday, two £1 notes, one 10s note and some silver. She always kept her purse anywhere in the kitchen. My portmanteau [also referred to as a Gladstone bag] was either in the disused room downstairs or in the lumber room upstairs . . .

On Sunday, she told me a man called to do the front garden. He asked her if he could do it up. She told me that she said she would not let him do it without my consent, as I always did it myself. I had already started to do the garden. I said to her, 'If he comes again, tell him I am going to do it myself.' I do not know what tradespeople call on a Monday morning. The milkman was there about 7.30 a.m. I think the washerwoman calls on a Monday morning and I think my wife was expecting a sewing woman to call. I do not know either of their names. I had the cloth on for breakfast this morning as usual. My wife said nothing further to me about the gardener, but she mentioned that she would not let him do it as she did not think much of him. My wife generally puts her black leather slippers (I think they had a strap on each) on in the morning. I think she changed them only when she wanted to go out.

The coal hammer, which has a sort of club head, is kept in the coal yard. My hatchet is nearly a new one. I have had it about six years [sic] but it has only done light work. It was not rusty; it was fairly new looking. I always keep it under the board where I keep the chips near the boiler. I generally break the chips on the mat at the back door. I use the axe myself and it is pretty sharp. I think they collect the laundry on a Tuesday. I wear flannel shirts and do not change every week. I did not change last week. So far as I could see, everything was as usual when I left home in the morning. My wife, so far as I know, has had no quarrel with anyone. I do not think she associated with anyone except the next door neighbour. My wife may have had stamps or other papers in her purse but I do not know. I took the milk in this morning. It was left at the door.

Hodgson was detained overnight and seen again the following day, after which he was charged under caution with the wilful murder of his wife and child. He was taken back to the house, where he was asked if he saw anything wrong with the scullery. Hodgson pointed to the blood on the floor and said 'That looks like it.' He also pointed out a bucket containing sticks for the fire, which had been overturned. He was then taken back to the cells to await the inquest.

At this time, Hodgson had not admitted any connection with the crime whatsoever. He had denied that the alleged murder weapon was his property, and had hinted, in further conversation with the police, that the portmanteau might have been filled by a burglar or murderer. There seemed to be no motive for the murder despite the occasional family argument, and neither was he short of money. There were, however, stains on his clothing which looked like blood, and the Wallasey police took no chances. A black overcoat, the chopper (*Exhibit* 3), a pair of blue serge trousers, waistcoat and coat, a pair of black boots and the famously unwashed striped shirt belonging to the arrested man were all sent off to none other than Bernard Spilsbury, fast becoming a world-famous pathologist, with a string of notable cases to his name.

The National Archive has his four-page report, handwritten in ink on foolscap paper, dated 21 April 1917 and countersigned by the magnificently named Bouverie J.P. McDonald, 'Committing Justice'. Included in the report were the following:

> Chopper – The head and greater part of the blade (except the edge) as well as the upper ⅔ of the handle show extensive reddish stains and splashes. These give the chemical reaction for blood. Several areas submitted to microscopical examination shew the presence of blood which has the character of human blood. . . . Several human hairs are adherent to the blood stains on the head of the chopper. Trousers . . . Two tiny red stains are situated near the end of the outer side of the left leg . . . there is a tiny clot on the outside of the right leg.'

The waistcoat, overcoat, left boot and blue serge coat all had bloodstains which Spilsbury reported as human, and his final conclusion was that 'On the chopper, the stains consist of human blood. On the blue serge suit and overcoat, the numbered stains are bloodstains . . . and resembling the blood on the chopper. On the left boot are stains which give the chemical reaction for blood but which have not been confirmed by microscopical examination.'

The area around Central Park Avenue was a hive of gossip, which rapidly spread along the Wirral and across the Mersey to Liverpool. Everyone seemed to be asking the same question: 'Why did he do it?' A possible explanation, and one that would send the area to even greater heights of speculation, was soon to surface. William Thomas Hodgson had a girlfriend!

Sarah Helena Llewellyn, known as Lena, lived with her parents, Thomas and Sarah, at 14 Mellor Road, Prenton, only just over a mile away from Robb Brothers. She was 29 and worked as a waitress and had first met Hodgson in a café at Easter 1916. Her statement included:

> He used to come into the café every day and we used to go for walks or to the pictures about twice a week. I did not know that he was married. I did not know that he lived in Liscard. The only address I had was Sutton House, where employees of Robb Brothers Ltd live in there. Shortly before Easter, my mother took me to a doctor in Liverpool. On the way back from Liverpool, we called at Robb Bros. My mother went in but I did not. The same night, he came up to our house and I and my mother had a conversation with him. We told him what the doctor had told him about my condition. I am going to have a child and I told the prisoner so . . . About April 4, I kept an appointment with him after receiving a letter [*Exhibit* 24a]. That was the first time I had seen him since the Friday we went to the pictures and I asked him to come up to our house as my mother wished to speak to him again. He was not very willing to come up. He did come and that was the last time I saw him until after April 16. My mother had a conversation with him and I joined in, subsequently. In [the] letter [*Exhibit* 25a] the coat was one I had asked him to get me to wear for the occasion. He paid for it. He has given me other presents. In between staying with my mother, I lodged at different places, including Manor Road [less than half a mile from Central Park Avenue]. I never told H. that I had lived in Manor Road nor any of the other places. I did not know until last Monday that H. was a married man. I did not know about Central Park Avenue until my mother went to Robb's on April 16.

It now became clear to the police that Hodgson had been placed in a severe dilemma. He was living a fairly settled life with his wife and family at Central Park Avenue, but for the last two years had also been enjoying a 'bit on the side' with Helena Llewellyn. It had not taken the girl's mother long to become suspicious of him; and once she found out that her daughter was pregnant, she was determined that Hodgson should do the right thing by her, as soon as possible. She had reminded him about this on one occasion at her home, when he replied petulantly, 'When I marry Lena, I shall not marry you', to which she had replied, 'I should not expect that.' By coincidence, she had intended to remind him again at Robb's on the actual date of the murder, when she called by only to be told that he was out at lunch.

With pressure being placed on him to name the day for the marriage, and knowing the utter impossibility of this, Hodgson knew that it would not be long before the entire affair would blow up in his face. He then risked the possibility of his wife leaving him, taking the children with her and suing for

Mellor Road, Prenton, where Helena Llewellyn lived with her parents. (Author)

divorce – something that would only spur on Mrs Llewellyn the more to insist that he now married Helena.

Who knows what passed between the Hodgsons on the fatal morning, but what is certain is that the Laws next door heard nothing, either of a row or the savage attack with the hatchet. Hodgson arrived late at work that morning, but there was nothing about him to suggest the awful events of the morning and a friend, Thomas Davies, would say in court that he had been sitting in the smoke room of a local public house on the evening of 16 April and had seen Hodgson there. Hodgson had said that he was going to have a drink and then go home and mind the baby while his wife and little girl went to the pictures, so even at that stage he was still trying to appear normal, although he must have realised by then that the bodies were almost certain to have been discovered.

On 18 April Hodgson was brought up before the magistrates at Liscard Court House, in front of Mr T. Raffles Bulley – there seems to have been no shortage of exotic forenames in that part of Cheshire! – charged with the killing of his wife and child. DI Pearson gave evidence of the arrest and charge, to which Hodgson had replied, 'Not Guilty', and the accused was then remanded for seven days.

Meanwhile, on 25 April, the coroner's inquest, conducted by Mr J.C. Bate, heard evidence presented by Mr G. Livesey, Deputy Town Clerk representing the Director of Public Prosecutions, with Hodgson being defended by Mr J.A. Behn, a well-known Liverpool solicitor. First of all the jury went to visit the scene of the crime, and afterwards, in his opening address, the coroner made reference to the portmanteau and told the jury that it was up to them to decide whether or not that was the effect of a bona fide robbery.

Dr Napier described to the court how he had found the bodies on 16 April and stated that cause of death was due to injury of the brain in both cases, combined with numerous fractures of the skull; and that those injuries were compatible with the hatchet labelled *Exhibit* 3. There were no signs of trauma other than to the head and the blows were extremely violent and had fractured nearly every bone in the skull in both cases. In his opinion, it had taken many heavy blows to cause those wounds.

Elsie May Todd, aged 12, gave evidence that she used to help Mrs Hodgson around the house each evening and on Saturdays. She knew that the tin money box was Netty's and that on 14 April Mrs Hodgson had emptied it using the blade of a knife and had counted about 14*s* in it before returning the coins to the box. She had seen the axe kept under the draining board in the scullery.

Sarah Llewellyn told the court that she had asked Hodgson, 'Do you intend being more than a friend to my daughter?', and had received the reply, 'Under present circumstances, I must.' 'I asked him if he was prepared to take my daughter and he replied, "I will stand by her and not leave her, don't worry." I told him that if he was a gentleman of honour, I should leave it to him as a gentleman. I saw him again on the Wednesday before Good Friday [4 April] and I asked him if he was prepared to take my daughter at Easter, and he told me, 'I cannot, for reasons of my own.' He never told me he was a married man and the first I knew of it was when three detectives called on 17 April.'

The Chief Constable, Percy Barry, told the court about the interview he had held with Hodgson, which was partly in answer to questions and partly through volunteered statements. 'The prisoner has never, to my knowledge, been asked to say what he had to say about the spots of blood on his clothing', he reported – obviously, the policeman did not know that Hodgson had already explained that he had cut himself shaving some time before 16 April. He also told the inquest that Hodgson, on being told officially for the first time that his wife and daughter were dead, had asked the chief constable to telegraph his father-in-law and brother-in-law telling them that his wife had 'passed away', and not to say anything about the child as his father-in-law 'would go mad if he knew'.

The coroner, in his summing-up, said that if Hodgson held the only key to the front door of no. 16, which he slammed to when he left in the morning, it was difficult to know how anybody else could have got in. This was a careless mistake on a vital piece of evidence – the police knew from statements that the front door was open when Mrs Law had knocked on the glass surround on the fatal evening. The coroner added that the evidence of Miss Llewellyn was not strong enough to prove a motive for the murders – a curious conclusion, seeing that Helena's mother had been breathing down Hodgson's neck.

The jury were out for a mere 20 minutes and returned with a verdict of murder against William Thomas Hodgson. During the whole of the hearing, Hodgson had been sitting with his head in his hands so that his face could not be seen over the walls of the dock. When the courtroom had been cleared, he was taken to Liverpool Prison.

At the resumed magistrates' hearing on 27 April, in answer to the charge of murder Hodgson replied, 'As I stand committed already for trial by the coroner on this terrible charge, no purpose would be served by me giving evidence today, but I will say again that I am not guilty. Nobody knows better than I the wrong I did in the relations with the girl Llewellyn, which commenced during the time before my wife and children came to live with me at Liscard, but the idea of committing this crime on her account is too absurd for anyone to believe. She knew I was married from the start. The only blood found upon my clothes must have proceeded from the cut which bled so severely when I was shaving. I do not wish to call any witnesses now.'

On 11 July, Hodgson faced trial at Chester Assizes before Mr Justice Avory. Mr Ellis Griffiths KC, MP, and Mr Trevor Lloyd appeared for the Crown, and Hodgson was defended by Mr Lindon Riley and Mr Ralph Sutton.

While in prison, Hodgson had written to a Mr George at Robb's, as follows:

> Dear Mr George,
> I suppose you have heard more of my trouble than I can tell you. I wrote to Benn [*sic*] and Co., Solicitors, Dale Street, [later Behn Twyford & Co.] asking them to call and see me here for my defence and should be pleased if you will be good enough to ring them up and find out if they are defending me and if not would you be kind enough to send a Birkenhead solicitor to see me. Well, Mr George, I suppose I have some money to receive from the firm . . . and shall be glad if you would forward me £6 to the following address for the benefit of the child [Cyril], the remainder I can have when I return, if I am fortunate enough to do so. Address Mrs Smith [his mother-in-law], 4 Amos Street, Moston, Manchester.

Five letters from Hodgson to Helena were produced as exhibits, all written on lined notepaper in pencil and headed 'Sutton House, Oliver Street, Birkenhead'.

Exhibit 22b dated 24 March 1917 read:

> My Dearest Lena, I promised I would write to you but really I have had very little to say to you only I am worried to death about you because I think your mother mistrusts me. I believe she thinks I am going to leave you. I am not and if you have the patience to wait until after Easter, we will make some arrangement so don't you worry, you will be alright. You will be with me before very long and then I think we shall both be satisfied and your mother too. Best love and kisses, your ever loving boy, Tom.

Exhibit 25a dated 10 April 1917 read:

> My dear Lena, I thought I would come up and see you tonight but I don't feel over grand and have not been well all the week end. I have been to the doctor and he has given me some awful stuff to take . . . How is the coat for you I sent up? Is it alright? Best love, your ever loving TH.

The final letter in the series was dated 14 April 1917, only two days before the murder, and read:

> My Dear Lena, I was sorry I could not get down last night. I was glad to get into bed and I am no better today and if I am no different on Monday, I shall not come next week at all, they will have to manage in my Dept., and I don't suppose the firm will thank me any more for it . . .
> Hoping you are keeping better,
> Best love and kisses from your ever loving boy Tom.

It was obvious from these letters that Hodgson was trying every excuse not to visit his pregnant mistress, and her mother's redoubtable appearance in court probably struck the jury as the reason why!

Bernard Spilsbury gave his evidence and described in detail the bloodstains on the hatchet and on Hodgson's clothing and boots. Modern methods and DNA testing would have shown in a short time whether the bloodstains on Hodgson's clothing belonged to his wife and child, but in 1917 this was simply not possible. In the gap between committal and trial, on 15 June, Lena Llewellyn had given birth to a child, whom she registered as Arthur Llewellyn. Not surprisingly, she left the name of the father blank on the birth certificate. She admitted in court that Hodgson was the father, but when she was asked if and when she had known that her lover was a married man, she prevaricated. Mr Riley, for the prosecution, asked a long series of questions on this point, but neither he nor the judge could persuade her to say anything. At length, Riley asked, 'Do you remember saying anything before the coroner that you only knew Hodgson was married yesterday, April 24?' Lena answered in a low voice, 'Yes.' 'Was that true?', and the court waited for the reply, 'No, Sir.' Mr Justice Avory now intervened and asked, 'Now you admit that was untrue, could you give us the truth now, once and for all.'

Once more, there was no answer.

Riley then asked, 'When you and Hodgson were at New Brighton last August, did he point out to you Central Park Avenue as the place where he was staying with his wife and family?' There was a long pause, and then the reply, 'I am not prepared to say that I did not know that he was a married man!'

Hodgson then went into the box and confirmed the facts of his age, employment and family details. He said that he had first met Helena Llewellyn in the middle of July 1916 and that 'impropriety' had taken place. He had told her he was a married man and insisted that he had pointed out Central Park Avenue as the place where he and his family were to live. He denied ever having laid a finger on his wife, although he admitted that she did not like him drinking. The reason why he had told Mrs Llewellyn that he could do nothing until Easter was that he was expecting a sum of money from Robb Brothers and would be able to give some to Helena 'to help her out with her trouble'.

CERTIFIED COPY OF AN ENTRY OF BIRTH

GIVEN AT THE GENERAL REGISTER OFFICE

Application Number COL 497295

REGISTRATION DISTRICT Birkenhead

1917 BIRTH in the Sub-district of Tranmere in the Counties of Birkenhead C.B. &c

Columns:-	1	2	3	4	5	6	7	8	9	10
No.	When and where born	Name, if any	Sex	Name and surname of father	Name, surname and maiden surname of mother	Occupation of father	Signature, description and residence of informant	When registered	Signature of registrar	Name entered after registration
206.	Fifteenth June 1917. 56. Church Road. Tranmere. U.D.	Arthur.	Boy	—	Sarah Helena Llewellyn. Café Waitress, of 14. Mellor Road. Tranmere. U.D.	—	S. H. Llewellyn. Mother. 56. Church Road. Tranmere.	Twenty-second June 1917.	S. W. Swan. Registrar.	

CERTIFIED to be a true copy of an entry in the certified copy of a Register of Births in the District above mentioned.

Given at the GENERAL REGISTER OFFICE, under the Seal of the said Office, the 20th day of January 2005

BXCA 777138

CAUTION: THERE ARE OFFENCES RELATING TO FALSIFYING OR ALTERING A CERTIFICATE AND USING OR POSSESSING A FALSE CERTIFICATE ©CROWN COPYRIGHT

WARNING: A CERTIFICATE IS NOT EVIDENCE OF IDENTITY.

GENERAL REGISTER OFFICE ENGLAND

031998 8281 10/04 SPSL 009195

SC

Birth certificate of Arthur Llewellyn. Note absence of father's name. (Crown copyright)

'Were you fond of this girl?' the accused was asked.

'Not particularly.'

'Were you in love with her?'

A pause, and then, 'No.'

Hodgson went on to say that the girl's mother had regarded him as merely keeping company with her daughter and he had had no intention of marrying her, whatever her mother had thought. He did not admit now, nor had he ever accepted, that Lena's baby was his.

What effect this brief exchange had on Helena, sitting only a few feet away, is not recorded, but the poor girl must have been shocked and sickened by the abrupt way in which Hodgson dismissed their two-year relationship and, more importantly, his callous manner cannot have escaped the attention of the judge and jury.

On Friday, Mr Griffith reviewed the case for the prosecution and placed heavy emphasis on the letters that Hodgson had written to his girlfriend – 'More lies than leaves', he called them; 'The letters were crammed with falsehoods.' 'All indications', he continued, 'pointed to the fact that

Rex v William Thomas Hodgson

Exhibit, 27A
[illegible] D. P. McDonald
Committing Justice

Sutton House
Oliver St

My Dear Lena
I was sorry I could not get down last night I was really glad to get into bed & I am no better today & if I am no different on Monday I shall not come next week at all, they will have to manage in my Dep^t I dont suppose the firm will thank me [illegible] any more for it however I will let you know how I am on Monday if I cannot get down at night hope you are keeping better

Best Love & Kisses
Your ever loving Boy
Tom

14th April 1917

Letter from Hodgson to his girlfriend. Note the address. (National Archives)

Mrs Hodgson was killed while in the act of making breakfast.' The fact that the beds were not made and baby Cyril was still in his cot led one to the conclusion that the deed had been done before Mrs Law had heard the vestibule door slam, as Hodgson left for work. He pointed out that on the night of the murder, despite the crowd round his own house and the police and ambulance vehicles, Hodgson had not gone straight in, but instead had gone to Mrs Law's next door. 'Was that the action of an innocent man?'

In his defence, Mr Riley said that Hodgson's demeanour on the day of the murder was calm and none of his workmates had noticed anything peculiar about him, nor had anyone noticed the so-called bloodstains on his clothing. Counsel pointed out to the jury that the blood on Hodgson's boots might well have got there when he walked into the kitchen and that the stains on Hodgson's clothing were very small and did not fit in with the fact that blood had been found on the walls to a height of approximately 7ft. No evidence had been brought to prove that the stains had not come from a shaving cut, nor a bloody nose, excuses that Hodgson had put forward to the police.

It is, indeed, peculiar that neither Spilsbury nor anyone else seems to have attempted to discover the blood group of the stains or sought to match them with Hodgson's own blood group. Blood grouping had been discovered seventeen years earlier by Dr Karl Landsteiner; the science was well enough advanced to have rendered this possible and might have solved the question once and for all.

Mr Riley's speech lasted exactly 2 hours, after which the court adjourned for lunch. Resuming when the court reconvened, Mr Justice Avory took the jury over the evidence in his usual painstaking way, reminding them that if there was any doubt in their minds that Hodgson had committed these terrible crimes, he was entitled to the benefit of it.

The jury were only absent for 14 minutes, and returned with a verdict of 'Guilty'. Putting on the black cap, the judge told Hodgson, 'I will not add to the pain of your present position by any observation of mine on the character of the crime of which you have been convicted, I am but the instrument of the law to pronounce upon you the sentence.' This he quickly proceeded to do, and it was noticed that the accused faced this ordeal with his usual stoic calm.

Had he not had a mistress, or had his demeanour in the dock not been so much against him, Hodgson might well have been found 'not guilty'. An appeal failed and he went to the scaffold at 9 a.m. on 16 August 1917 at Liverpool Prison, where he was given a drop of 6ft 4in by John Ellis and was dead within 30 seconds of being taken from the condemned cell. Only a handful of people waited outside the prison gate to see the sign that the law had exacted the full penalty.

Opposite: Extract from Cheshire Courier. (Cheshire Record Office)

in evidence that Hodgson had been keeping company with a young woman employed at a Birkenhead cafe. He had posed as a single man, and had had interviews with the girl's mother as to her condition, promising not to leave her in the lurch.

Coroner's Statement.

Mr. G. Livsey, Deputy Town Clerk, represented the Director of Public Prosecutions, and Hodgson was represented by Mr. J. A. Bohn, solicitor, Liverpool.

At the outset of the proceedings, upon the suggestion of the Coroner, the jury went to view the scene of the tragedy.

In his opening statement the Coroner said Margaret Alderson Hodgson (37) and her daughter, three years of age, were the wife and daughter of Thomas William Hodgson. They had resided at Liscard since August 1st last, prior to which they lived at Huddersfield.

Referring to the evidence that was to be given to the jury, the Coroner said on April 10th a neighbour who had been in the habit of seeing Mrs. Hodgson, and whose little girl played with the deceased child, missed them during the day. At about six o'clock in the evening she was letting some friends out of her house, and knocked at the panel of the door of deceased's house.

She received no reply, so went to the vestibule door, which was partly open. She opened it and called, but heard nothing except the crying of a child upstairs.

She went into the house, and in the back kitchen found Mrs. Hodgson and the child lying on the floor. She was startled, and immediately called in a man who was passing. They went into the house together and sent for the police and ambulance. The jury would notice spots of blood on part of the scullery walls, and also spots of blood on the clothing of the husband.

Referring to the motive of the alleged murder, the Coroner said there was a portmanteau containing several articles in the dining-room. Upon hearing the evidence it was for them to decide whether or not that was the effect of a bona-fide robbery. Were these goods placed there by some person who intended to carry them away? One thing was evident: that whoever placed them there would be the person guilty of the crime committed.

Husband and Another Woman.

The Coroner also referred to the fact that the husband, Wm. Thos. Hodgson, had been keeping company with a woman in Birkenhead since April last up to about Christmas. She did not know that he was married, and the evidence would show that she was in a certain condition, and that the man Hodgson was the father.

Dr. Napier, the police surgeon, was the first witness. He described the condition of the victims' bodies, which he saw on the night of the tragedy. The faces of both were much blood-stained. There was a large quantity of blood on the floor and brain substance near the woman's head. The child's head was also surrounded by blood, and here again was brain substance.

The skulls of both had been fractured, with fragments of bone protruding. There were spots of blood on the wall. Lying on the floor he observed a hatchet (produced). On the blunt side of the blade there were bloodstains which were also present along four inches of the handle.

Dr. Napier went on to say that there were also hairs adhering to the blade of the hatchet. There was no evidence of a struggle, and he considered that the bodies had been dead for several hours, probably eight or ten. On a wicker chair in the kitchen was a child's doll.

Witness described the post-mortem examination he made of the woman's body, and said there must have been many blows of great violence used to have caused such injuries to the head. From his examination of the stomach, which contained no food, he was of opinion that the woman had not consumed any food for at least ten or twelve hours before death, which he considered occurred early on Monday morning. There was no sign of disease in any portion of the body, and he considered death was the result of injuries to the brain and numerous fractures of the skull. These injuries were, in his opinion, compatible with such as could be inflicted with the hatchet he found near the bodies.

Dealing with his post-mortem on the body of the child, Dr. Napier said there was much blood on the back and the right side of the head, and also escaping from the ear. Those on the child's head must have been several in number and violent in character, and were, in his opinion, caused by the same hatchet as that used on the woman. The stomach was practically empty, and he considered no food had been consumed by the girl since the previous evening.

He was of opinion that death was the result of direct violence causing serious injury to the brain and skull.

The Coroner.—Would one blow from the hatchet probably cause unconsciousness? Yes, I think so.

understood he meant to marry her daughter.

On April 4th, when she again saw him at the house, she said to him, "You have been my daughter's downfall, and you are the only man who can lift her." He replied he could not do anything before Easter, and said, "When I marry Lena I shall not marry you." She answered, "I do not expect that." She first heard he was married a week ago.

In reply to Mr. Livsey, witness said that since Christmas her daughter had been ill, and Hodgson had seen her a few times.

Mr. Livsey.—In her bedroom? Yes.

Mrs. Westmore, 15, Central Park-avenue, said she saw Wm. Thomas Hodgson on Monday, 10th April, leaving his house about nine

WM. THOMAS HODGSON.

(Sketched at the inquest).

o'clock in the morning. She at first heard the door "bang," and when Hodgson came out he was carrying a small parcel.

Florence Starke, in the employ of Messrs. Robb Bros., Birkenhead, in the same department as William Thomas Hodgson, deposed that on the day the crime was discovered Hodgson arrived at work about 25 minutes past nine. She noticed nothing unusual about him during the morning, but when he returned from lunch and she told him that Miss Llewellyn's mother had been to the shop, he seemed vexed. On several occasions witness had noticed that he seemed worried, and muttered to himself. On the Monday afternoon he looked agitated, and said he had a headache. Until the calling of Mrs. Llewellyn he was perfectly calm and acted just as usual.

By a Juror.—It was not unusual for Hodgson to arrive at work late.

Unhappy Married Life.

Joseph Robinson, of Leeds, brother-in-law of the deceased woman, Mrs. Hodgson, said he had known William Thomas Hodgson about ten years. He knew that she and Hodgson had frequent quarrels on account of the late hours that he kept, and they did not live happily together. Witness and his wife visited them at Liscard during last Easter week-end, and they seemed to be on better terms, though on one or two occasions they had a slight quarrel because he stayed out rather long when on an errand. Hodgson did not sleep with his wife that week-end, but that was nothing unusual. He was not a sober man, but frequently was the worse for drink, and then he had a "bad temper." When not drunk he seemed a man who would cause trouble when there was not occasion, and witness did not remember visiting them on a single occasion when there wasn't a quarrel.

By Mr. Bohn.—They quarrelled over paltry matters.

William Smith, an estate agent, 4, Amos-street, Morton, Manchester, the father of Margaret Alderson Hodgson, deposed that Hodgson and his daughter were married about six or seven years ago, and since then accused had been in a considerable number of situations. At times they lived happily together, but sometimes were very disagreeable indeed. Hodgson had a very ungovernable temper, especially when under the influence of drink. Mrs. Hodgson was a little hasty, but she was of an amiable and lovable disposition.

By a Juror.—He had known of occasions when Hodgson "knocked his wife about," and from what Mrs. Hodgson had said it must have been frequent.

By Another Juror.—Mrs. Hodgson was not jealous of him and did not accuse him of being unfaithful to her.

Witness added:—I opposed the marriage and pleaded with her to come home, but she tried to make the best of it.

10

THE LOSER

Bramhall, 1922

Frederick George Wood was one of life's losers. Although he came from a decent family, he had made nothing of his life and by the age of 28 was reduced to roaming the north of England, going from door to door begging for casual work. Invalided out of the First World War in 1917, after being wounded in action, he now had a damaged left forearm. This, however, did not prevent him from working as a furniture upholsterer, and he was following this occupation when, in 1922, he found himself in Bramhall.

At the centre of the prosperous middle-class village was a road junction, from where Ack Lane ran north-west towards Cheadle Hulme and within yards of the start of Ack Lane, Moss Lane ran off on the left, within a few hundred yards dividing again to become Acre Lane. Here, within the last few years, some substantial properties had been built.

One such was Invermay, a detached four-bedroomed house with a gabled end facing the road, but with the actual entrance on the left-hand side of the house, just before a small, brick-built garage. The downstairs accommodation consisted of entrance and hall, with a dining-room to the right and a somewhat over-furnished sitting-room to the left, in addition to kitchen, scullery, larder, coals and WC.

Here lived Mr John White, a cashier with the York Street, Manchester branch of the London County and Westminster Bank, and his 50-year-old sister Margaret Gilchrist White, a spinster who had been keeping house for her brother since the death of their mother. The house was comfortable and the siblings got on well, sharing breakfast each weekday before Mr White walked to the station to catch his train to the city. When he came home at around 6 p.m., Margaret always had a meal waiting for him.

During the day, she busied herself with general housework, sometimes chatting with her next-door neighbour Mrs Fanny Pye, the wife of an architect. The houses were quite close together and the two women, if not exactly friends, knew one another well. Margaret White had an Irish terrier named Bruin to keep her company, an excitable creature who barked furiously if anyone rang the doorbell and who she would generally shut in the kitchen if someone called. The sitting-room, to the left of the entrance door, looked

Acre Lane, Bramhall. (Author)

out over a nursery garden. The room itself was rather cramped because of the considerable amount of furniture it contained, including a sideboard, buffet, bureau, bookcase and drawers, three tables, a couch and five chairs. John White was well aware that his sister was very particular about the furnishings in the house, although she rarely did any remedial work herself, preferring to use local tradesmen. The house was lit by gas all the way through.

Margaret White usually enjoyed good health, but some months before she had been advised to get away for two or three months to avoid a nervous breakdown. When she returned she engaged the services of Mrs Florence Hill, who came two days a week, Wednesdays and Fridays, to help with the housework, the two ladies usually having their lunch together at about 12.30 p.m.

On Monday 18 December 1922, Mr White left for work as usual and returned a little later than normal at about 6.40 p.m. By then the sun had gone down, and as he walked down the side of the house towards the front door he observed that the house was in darkness, which was unusual. Going straight through the hall into the kitchen and finding no one there, he turned into the sitting-room and stumbled over something on the floor. Fumbling about with his hands in the darkness, he felt the cold form of a body and, after hastily turning on the gas, found to his horror that it was that of his sister. Margaret White lay on her back fully dressed, her feet towards the door, her arms crossed over her face and a grey alpaca apron drawn round the upper part of her shoulders. Despite his inexperienced touch, her brother could tell she was dead.

Mr White tried to move his sister's hands, but found it impossible to do so; and by now in a very agitated state, he took out his penknife and attempted to cut the apron from around her neck. Realising that this would do no good, he ran out to the house of Mrs Whiteley, who lived on the opposite side to Mrs Pye. 'There's something very wrong next door', he stuttered. 'Could you please telephone for the doctor?' The bemused Mrs Whiteley did as she was asked and within a few minutes Dr Andrew Thomson arrived, to find John White trying to give his sister artificial respiration. Moving White gently aside, he felt for a pulse, which was absent, and then moved to close the dead woman's legs, which were spread apart. He had difficulty with this because of the advancing rigor mortis, which was enough to confirm that Miss White was dead and had been so for some 7 or 8 hours. He noted the apron round her neck, cut where John White had tried and failed to release it, and he carefully disentangled the piece of cloth. Considering that there was nothing more that he could do, he turned to leave, advising John White that he should call the police and cautioning him not to touch the body again until they arrived. Mr White went back to the Whiteleys and telephoned the local police station, and at the same time, contacted the cleaner, Mrs Hill, who arrived at about 7 p.m. The kitchen window was open and she knew that the sash cords were broken and that the window was usually kept open by a piece of wood. Her first instinct was to put the kettle on. Going into the kitchen, she saw pieces of tapestry and some small tacks on the floor, to the right of the table.

Within minutes, Sergeant Walter Postons arrived. He looked round the house, accompanied by John White, and noted that there seemed to be no signs of a struggle. However, when they went into Miss White's bedroom, which was over the sitting-room, they found the room in a state of disorder. On the bed, a cash box and two other wooden boxes, formerly locked, had been forced open. Also on the bed was a leather satchel containing keys, which had been ripped open, and on the floor, between bed and dressing-table, lay a piece of webbing. Drawers in both dressing-tables were open, and on one was a case containing three rings, a lady's gold watch and some other jewellery. No money could be found in the house, even after a determined search, and on going into Mr White's bedroom Postons noted that an attempt had been made to force

Invermay. (Author's collection)

open a writing-slope, which lay on a bedside chair. Downstairs in the hall, about 2yd from the front door, he found a lady's black comb, while in the kitchen there was an enamel bowl in the sink containing a little water and some burnt linen.*

Mr White suddenly bent down and picked up from the floor a blue postcard, with some writing on it in pencil, which he then handed to the sergeant. It was just an ordinary postcard and written on it was a name and address: 'Fred Wood, c/o Mr Cooper, Church Street, Wilmslow'. 'Do you recognise the writing?' he asked. John White shook his head. 'I found it in the house a few days ago,' he said; 'I think it may be something to do with an ottoman that Margaret was getting repaired.' He pointed into the hall, where a small chair stood at the foot of the staircase. 'When I left for work this morning, that chair was in my bedroom. It looks to me as though it has been re-covered.' Postons put the postcard in his pocket, and then, ignoring police protocol, proposed that Miss White's body should be moved, which he accomplished with the help of Mrs Hill, who was obviously a lady of some character. Between them they struggled to lift the rapidly stiffening corpse and carry it upstairs to the late woman's bedroom, laying it on the bed. Having accomplished this task, Mrs Hill went into the kitchen to make another cup of tea. Aimlessly, John White followed her and bent down to pick up some pieces of tapestry lying on the floor. By now, other policemen were arriving, and in due course the corpse of Margaret White was removed to the local mortuary, leaving a distraught and bewildered John White alone with his thoughts.

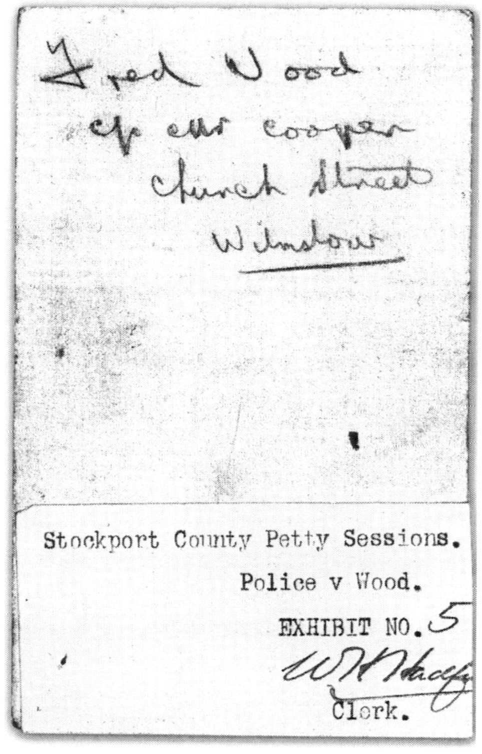
Fred Wood
c/o Mr Cooper
Church Street
Wilmslow

Stockport County Petty Sessions.
Police v Wood.
EXHIBIT NO. 5
Clerk.

Fred Wood's postcard. (National Archives)

On Wednesday 20 December, a post-mortem was conducted by Dr Roland Nightingale, assisted by Dr Henry George Anderson of Bramhall. In his deposition to the court, Dr Nightingale noted various marks and scratches on Miss White's arms and on her neck, where there was a considerable discolouration of the tissues, extending right round the neck to a depth of 2½in. Bruising was apparent round the left side of the lower jaw and the angle of the mouth. Under the lobes of both ears, he found well-marked points of echymoses (small dilated blood points caused by pressure and almost always

*The author has examined this material at the National Archives and considers that it is almost certainly the remains of a man's pocket handkerchief.

present in the soft tissue of the face and head in cases of strangulation). From the appearance of the marks round the neck, it looked as though Miss White had been seized round the throat by a person standing on her left-hand side. Considerable violence had been used and death would have ensued within 3 minutes, caused by throttling rather than a cord or ligature.

Judging from the fact that the stomach was empty and that there was partially digested food in the small intestine, he came to the conclusion that the deceased had had food that day and had lived for 3 or 4 hours after her last meal. Finally, he considered that all the marks had been made within the last 50 hours and that the injuries could not have been self-inflicted.

It is curious that Dr Nightingale made no mention of the hyoid bone, which is a U-shaped bone at the base of the tongue supporting the tongue muscles and fastened to either side of the skull. This arch-shaped bone is almost invariably broken in cases of manual strangulation, although the great pathologist Sir Bernard Spilsbury once gave evidence that this was not always the case. (Spilsbury was very much a law unto himself when at the height of his powers in the 1920s and '30s, and few dared to contradict his evidence in court.)

Dr Anderson, in his deposition, contented himself by saying that he did not agree with his colleague as to how the throttling was probably caused. His impression was that the deceased had been attacked from behind and gripped around the neck with both hands.

The Chief Constable of the Cheshire force, Major (later Lieutenant-Colonel) Pulteney Malcolm, was now faced with an awkward decision. Few of the provincial police forces of the time had the manpower or the experience to conduct murder inquiries, and Cheshire was no exception. He could allow his own men to proceed with the case and hope for the best, or he could call for assistance from Scotland Yard. In the latter case, he had only a few hours in which to make the decision, otherwise his force would have to carry the whole cost of the investigation. If the Yard were called in without delay, they carried their own expenses. Thus it was that Chief Inspector William Brown journeyed to Bramhall on 20 December, accompanied by Sergeant Baker, and together they examined Invermay throughout. Inspector Kingman of the Cheshire police joined them a day later.

The police quickly made enquiries at the address on the blue postcard and Mrs Annie Minnie Brehen (also known as Cooper) confirmed that she had recently put up a guest calling himself Frederick Wood, who had paid his rent up until 17 December. He had then left, leaving his bed unslept in, and she had not seen him since. On interviewing the other residents of the lodging-house, the police were pointed in the direction of Peter Gately and a lady whom he sometimes referred to as 'the wife', but who in reality was Ellen Middleton. What Gately had to tell the police and later put into a written statement galvanised them into action. Gately said that he was an unemployed iron-and-steel worker and he knew a Fred Wood, who had stayed at the same lodging-house. Wood was an upholsterer by trade, and in possession of a disability pension of 12s a week. Wood had told Gately that he had been doing upholstery jobs in the neighbourhood and that he had a big job on with Mrs Wilhelmina Rosina Wood, who lived at Yew Tree Cottage, Ack Lane, Bramhall – people in the area must have found it confusing to have Ack Lane and Acre Lane within a few hundred yards of one another! The two men agreed to share the job and both went to Mrs Wood's house on Thursday 14 December. For some reason Mrs Wood was not ready for them, and so they returned next day and worked until darkness fell, at around 4 p.m. There was a couch and a chair to be reupholstered and Wood told Gately that Mrs Wood had bought all the materials herself and was just paying them for their labour. (It would appear that, for all his fecklessness, Fred Wood was a decent upholsterer, as there seems to have been no complaint about his work, even though the only tools he used were a hammer and a screwdriver.)

The two men returned to Ack Lane on the Saturday and worked until it got dark, but the job was still not finished. According to Gately, the hardest part of the job was stretching the webbing onto the frame of the couch. He did the stretching and Wood hammered in the tacks, during which Gately noticed that Wood could use the hammer with either hand. On the way to their lodgings that evening, Wood gave Gately a packet of cigarettes and 8*s* 4*d* on account, telling him that as there was only about 2 hours' work left on the job he would return on the Monday to finish it and would meet Gately and settle up with him.

On Monday 18 December, Wood told Gately that he was going to Mrs Wood's and would return at about 3 p.m. to 'fix him up', explaining that he was expecting to be paid £2 for the job. However, what he did not mention was that on the evening of the first day at Yew Tree Cottage, after leaving his assistant outside on some pretext, Wood had returned to the house and asked Mrs Wood for a sub. 'Not for me, you understand,' he had told the lady, 'but for my companion who has a wife and children to support.' Mrs Wood gave him £1 and he left to join his co-worker. On the second night, having again slipped away from Gately, Wood attempted to con a further amount 'on account' from Mrs Wood, who by now was feeling somewhat suspicious and a little angry that the job appeared to be dragging on. At first, she refused to pay anything more, at which Wood reached into his pocket and produced his pension book, which he said she could hold as security. 'Do you think I would jeopardise this for a few pounds?' he asked her, with a note of incredulity in his voice. His employer pushed it away. 'I don't want your book', she told him abruptly, and thrust a 10s note into his hand. Thanking her profusely, but keeping his voice down so that Gately would not hear, he left the house and walked home with his colleague. Gately, unaware of the two 'advances' that Wood had obtained, was also ignorant of the fact that Wood had no intention of returning to finish the job on the following Monday.

The police gave details of their wanted man, with a description as follows:

> Fred Wood, also known as Ronald Lee, 29 years old, 5ft 7½in tall, clean shaven, with brown eyes and dark hair. He has a crippled left forearm, due to a war wound, for which he is in receipt of a small pension, and there are tattoo marks on his arms and chest.

On Thursday 21 December, the inquest on Margaret White opened at the Wesleyan Chapel Room, Bramhall. However, after evidence of identification of the body the hearing was swiftly adjourned by the coroner Mr Ferns until Thursday 4 January 1923 at 2 p.m., Mr Ferns explaining that there were several matters in connection with the case that made it desirable that the police should be able to work unhampered by any publication of the evidence. The jury was bound over in the sum of £10 to 'personally appear at the time and place fixed for further enquiry'.

Wood, having travelled first to Leeds, was now in Bradford, where he called on his mother, asking for money. She, no doubt having had enough of her deadbeat son, told him to go and see his brother, a respectable solicitor in the town, who gave him £2 and then ushered him out of his office in short order. Later that day, Wood took the train to Hull, where he stayed overnight, and by Friday 22 December he was in Grimsby. The next morning, he made his way to Lincoln where, after finding lodgings for the night, he entered a barber's shop. Sitting down to wait his turn, he picked up a newspaper and saw in it his name and description as a wanted man.

Wood's actions around the time of the murder were somewhat curious. He had diddled Peter Gately out of his rightful share of the Yew Tree Cottage money and had then quit the job, even though there was another 10s still to be drawn on it. His motive in leaving the area had presumably been prompted by his knowledge that an angry Gately would be on the lookout for him, but he had little money and what he did have was mostly used up in one aimless journey or another, plus the cost of lodgings. While there might have been some logic to his going to his family for money, there seems to have been little purpose in his other wanderings, which merely served to eat up his meagre store of cash.

Staring at the newspaper and realising that he was now officially on the run, with no money left, he decided to make his way to the police station and hand himself in to the police. He walked in and pointed to the newspaper description. 'That's me', he said to Detective Constable James Barker, and went on to protest that he had nothing whatsoever to do with the murder. 'I left Bramhall that Monday about 12 noon,' he told the constable, 'it's nothing to do with me.'

By 4 p.m. that day, Chief Inspector Brown and Inspector Kingman had arrived at Lincoln city police station and proceeded to interview Wood. Introducing himself, Brown said, 'I am Chief Inspector Brown and this is Inspector Kingman. I understand that you have stated to the police that you are the man circulated in the newspapers whose whereabouts we want to know in connection with a matter in Cheshire in Cheadle Hulme.' (The exact border of Bramhall/Cheadle Hulme was rather less defined in 1922 than it is now, owing to the more open situation of the area.) Wood replied, 'What else could I do? You have got every address in the papers where I am known. It says: Fred Wood, 5ft 7, tattoo marks on arms, grey suit. I couldn't go anywhere.'

'I should like you to give me a full account of all your movements on Monday 18 December', said Brown. Wood shrugged his shoulders. 'Yes, I will tell you.' The following is a résumé of his statement, with Wood's grammar uncorrected:

> This is the true and voluntary statement made by me Fred Wood concerning the 18th December 1922. I got up at the lodge about 9 o'clock, I then had breakfast. About 9.30, I got ready to go to Mrs Woods, Yew Tree Cottage, Ack Lane, Bramhall. On account of it raining I decided to wait until it had abated. About this time Peter Gately and his wife as I knew her had then gone. I, Fred Wood, did not [Wood's underlining] go out with them but waited till about 10.15 when it had ceased raining. I then left the lodge and went up to Handforth Road, walking until I got to the rough built cottages where I turned right to the footpath through the fields under the railway arch, through some more fields where I arrived at Padfield Cottages, Stanley Road, where I turned to the right to Bramhall. While walking up Stanley Rd, I decided on the spur of the moment to go home to see what could be done for me, it being so near Christmas. As I was walking along I emptied my pockets of tacks, also many odds and ends that I decided would be of no use to me in future. I did not call at any house nor had I any appointment to do so, otherwise than Mrs Woods, Yew Tree Cottage, Bramhall where up to that moment I decided to go. Going up Stanley Rd to the top of Acre Lane, the time being about 11.10, I had got about halfway down when a lady said, 'Good morning, Mr Wood.' I did not know the lady's name then. I went across as it was a lady I had worked for a week ago, repairing an Ottoman for which I received *9s 6d*. I did the work outside as the lady said the dog was so fierce. Before the lady paid me for the ottoman, she asked me for a few of my gimp pins (a kind of small tack). I gave her a handful of them, she who I now know to be Miss White stating that she could not afford to pay the upholsterer such a big price for doing her some chairs. Miss W. saying that after the instructions that I had given her that she would put the tapestry on herself seeing that she had some remnants of tapestry in the house somewhere.
>
> As I said, the lady said 'Good morning' and called me over. I went to her and she said at the Garden Gate [Wood's underlining], 'I have cut the pattern but do not know how to pleat it. If you will spare me a few moments, I will pay you for your trouble.' It being decided that I lend

her my tools also instruct her how to do it, she doing the work. I would receive 2*s* 6*d* for my trouble. I agreed on account of Miss White being so kind with me as regards the ottoman. Miss White told me to wait at the garden gate till she fastened the dog up. I then went to the front door. I standing on the top step. Miss White working just inside the Hall on my instructions. I told Miss White how to do it and she done it according to her idea quite satisfactorily. The chair being finished, she said, 'Thank you very much. I shall be able to repair my own work now, but won't it spoil you getting work again if you tell everyone how to do their own work?' I said, 'No, as I do not stay in one district long enough.' Miss White then said, 'Wait a moment, Mr Wood, and I will pay you', handing me my tools which composed of a screwdriver and small hammer. She went upstairs then, I still standing on the doorstep, she returned, coming downstairs with an enamel bowl in her hands turning to the right at the bottom of the stairs as if to me she was going into the room, I could not see the room then on account of the door being half closed. I heard a noise of the bowl dropping. I waited a moment thinking she had just dropped it and after probably a few seconds I heard a groan. With a noise of the bowl dropping one second and then hearing a groan I got frightened so I put my head in after pushing the door open and saw Miss White lying on the floor clutching at her throat, her face to my idea at the same time changing colour. I thought she was in a fit. I of course being frightened went in to her and tried to get her hands free from her throat she was very strong and I not being strong and ill it took me all my time to get her hands from her throat. I have a broken arm and could not hold them down so kneeling on one and holding the other with my good hand I tied them with something which I cannot remember I being very frightened on account of then being alone in the house with Miss White, I tried to revive her by rubbing her hands and holding her head up. Miss W. appeared to me to be very bad, she groaning and rolling her head

Site of the 'rough built' cottages. (Author)

about. Being frightened at being in the house and in all probability no one seeing me or hearing our conversation at the garden gate I went queer and having only 12*s* 6*d* of my own then I dashed upstairs, why I did not know at the time. I saw some boxes, broke them open and got about 15s came downstairs. Miss W. was then breathing very heavy as if in an anaesthetic I knowing the sounds on account of my being in hospital. Still frightened and in an excited state I come out and shut the door. The dog barked once after that. I come down Acre Lane got some cigs at a shop and then got a bus for Stockport as regards the time I could not swear to. I got the train to Leeds where I got lodgings for the night and going out at night time I saw someone that had been in hospital with me. Told him I was out of work and he got me some money from himself and a few of his friends I should think about 17s. I got up next morning and went to Middlesborough to see my sister. I returned to Leeds the same day, got lodging for the night. Next morning I went to Bradford that was on Wednesday 20 December. I went to my mother's house she saying go see your brother at the office. I went, saw him, asked him for some money and he gave me £2. About noon on the same day, I took the train to Hull stayed the night. On Thursday I took the ferry to New Holland then train to Grimsby stayed the night that was Friday 22 December. Next morning I walked part and rode part of the way to Lincoln where I arrived about 5 p.m. I went and got lodgings and tea then went to a barbers shop. Seeing a full description of myself in the daily paper I went to the police station at Lincoln and gave myself up for the description that was published as regards the person called Fred Wood. That is about all that I remember clearly but I say quite clearly that I Fred Wood did not kill Miss White, the other things happening in my frightened and excited condition what I had just wrote. This is a perfectly true description of what occurred on the 18 December and up to me giving myself up at Lincoln.

This long and rambling explanation was far from satisfactory so far as the police were concerned and, abandoning thoughts of Christmas lunch with their respective families, Brown and Kingman returned the following morning at 9 a.m. and told Wood that they were not satisfied with the statement he had made. Staring hard at Wood, Chief Inspector Brown said, 'The dead body of Miss Margaret Gilchrist White was found in her home in Acre Lane, Cheadle Hulme on Monday 18 December and you may be charged with her murder.' Brown then proceeded to caution Wood, who muttered, 'I'll say nowt.'

Wood was then taken to Cheadle police station, and on the way there he remarked, 'I have never been in this part of Cheadle Hulme before, only the Bramhall side. If you would like to take me there, I will show you where I threw my tools. I dropped them just over the hedge as I was walking on the footpath.' Arriving in Acre Lane, Wood pointed to a field just along the road from Invermay, which was searched with no result. Eventually, Wood was taken back to Cheadle Hulme Police Station for the night.

On 26 December, Wood was again confronted by the policemen and told that the hammer and screwdriver had now been found by Constable Wilfred Bowyer. Wood remarked, 'I suppose this is the capital charge for me? What reason have you got for it?' He was shown a piece of webbing and told that it had been found in Miss White's bedroom and was identical to a piece that he had used to repair furniture at Yew Tree Cottage. It was also pointed out to him that a chair that had been found standing in the hall at Invermay looked as though it had only been re-upholstered that day (18 December).

Wood replied, 'Ah, that would take an hour to do. Now it's up to me to prove I hadn't got time to do it as I went by the 11.30 a.m. bus from the Victoria Hotel and waited at Stockport for the 1.37 train, which I had to wait about an hour for.'

Brown pointed out that the packing under the cover of the chair was similar to some found in a bundle which had been recovered from the lodging-house at Wilmslow. Wood was then again cautioned and charged with the murder of Miss White, to which he replied, 'I know nothing about it at all.'

Taken to Stockport police station by CI Brown and Inspector Kingman, Wood remarked, 'Now I've got to fight you on time. I want you to find a nurse who was with some children with hair like mops who were standing outside the Victoria Hotel when I got on the bus at 11.30, also two men who were in the same bus as me, talking about the sale of a motor car. The driver will remember me as well, because after we left the Victoria he had to pull up for two ladies who came running down a drive, and he joked that he would have to charge them for waiting.'

The witness transcripts at the National Archives show that Nurse Emmie Baker confirmed that she had charge of two children with frizzy hair and a 'rather unusual appearance', although she did not elaborate on this. She was standing near the Victoria Hotel and saw the 12.30 bus come in. She denied that she had seen the 11.30 bus either in or out.

Elsie Freda Thorpe said that she had left Thornton, Park Road, Cheadle Hulme in the company of her friend on 18 December at 12.30 and had to flag the bus driver down, as they were late.

James Pearson Chapman confirmed that he had been talking about a motor car on the 12.30 bus, and the bus driver, Walter Harrison, remembered joking with the two ladies.

It was clear to the police that Wood was trying to place himself on the bus an hour earlier than the one he actually caught, although why he should have expected to get away with such a simple lie is not clear. From Stockport, Wood was taken to Manchester (Strangeways) Prison and remained there until the deferred inquest was reopened on 4 January 1923, which he attended in the custody of two warders. Before the hearing started, which merely deferred the inquest yet again, Wood asked for writing paper and wrote a five-page statement largely agreeing with the one taken down by CI Brown on 24 December although now stating that he could not swear to the time of the bus to Stockport. He then sealed it in a blue envelope and wrote on the front, 'To Mr Brown. Not to be opened till after the inquest. F.W.' Needless to say, Brown opened the envelope the minute it was passed on to him by Sergeant Postons.

Wood's trial took place at Chester Castle on 26 February 1923, but for some weeks before he had been making life difficult for his defence team, led by his solicitor Mr Barlow. Wood was now making great play of the fact that he had a damaged left arm, which he claimed would have made it impossible for him to have strangled Miss White in the way that Dr Nightingale had described. A précis of Wood's medical history at the National Archives discloses that on 9 November 1917 he was wounded in the left forearm by rifle fire, 'the bullet causing a through-and-through wound with much destruction of bone at exit'.

In October 1918, there was still an 'ununited fracture of the ulna in its lower 3rd and a gap in the bone of about one inch. Grip weakened 50%'. Three years later, a bone graft operation was performed and it was reported that as a result of treatment, massage, grafting and 'Faradism' (electric treatment), the left forearm was 'stronger'. In October 1922, Wood had further treatment at Grangethorpe Hospital, Manchester. It was then stated that the bone graft was soundly united at the lower end, but that the upper was 'broken and ununited'. He was recommended as an urgent case for a further operation on 30 October, but failed to turn up at the hospital for it.

Wood now started a barrage of correspondence including letters to the Home Office demanding, 'In the interest of my defence, also Justice, I ask you to grant me two [Wood's underlining] or more fully qualified doctors. They must be attached to the Civil Service, Police Force or Ministry of Pensions, to give me a most strict and searching examination re. physical disability and general condition [Wood had lost more than 2 stones in weight while awaiting his trial].' After consideration, the Home Office decided that they would pay for the cost of a single doctor. They also recommended that Wood should apply for legal aid, something that he had previously declined to do. On 9 February this was still his position, and the Home Office decided that the trial judge would probably order that legal aid be granted if the accused was still intransigent by the time the trial started.

On 19 February, Wood wrote to his brother:

> Dear Kid
> Well as regards my defence up to now there is none or rather anything that has been committed to paper. I have wrote re depositions so as to be able to put a defence in a proper manner but up to now nothing doing. *In fact I believe they are purposefully holding back any facilities that can be*

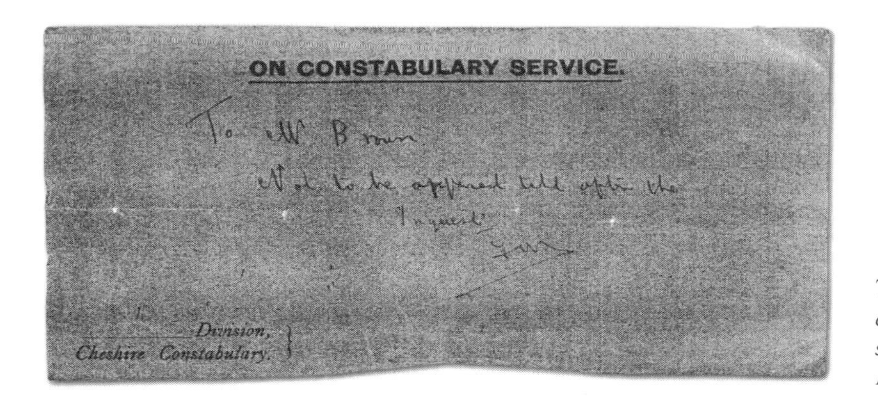

The envelope which contained Wood's further statement. (National Archives)

X-ray, showing damage to Wood's arm. (National Archives)

granted me [Author's italics]. I am not going to worry but I shall speak to reason when I get tried. You may be sure there will be a row in that dock.

By the date of the trial, Wood had at last sorted out his defence arrangements, having accepted the services of a Stockport solicitor, Mr E. Barlow, and a young lawyer, Mr Goodman Roberts. The trial, which lasted three days, opened in front of Mr Justice Swift, with Ellis Griffith KC leading for the prosecution, assisted by Mr Austin Jones.

Wood's main defence was that he could not have strangled Miss White because of the long-standing injury to his left forearm. *Exhibit* 34 at the trial comprised a précis of his medical history, from the gunshot wound received in 1917, through various inspections and bone grafts. A report dated 20 April 1922 noted that there was considerable wasting of the muscle of his left forearm and that his grip was weak. Wood was admitted to Beckett's Park Hospital, Leeds, in June 1922, when the wire was removed from the old bone graft. His general condition was by then 'fairly good', and although further surgery was needed and arrangements were made, again Wood failed to attend.

Drs Nightingale and Anderson agreed that Miss White had been strangled, but both had differing versions of how the attacker had done it. Nightingale told the court that he had examined Wood's arm and was of the opinion that he was strong enough to have strangled Miss White.

Wood gave evidence, basically a repeat of his statement, and claimed that Miss White had been alive and breathing heavily when he had left the house in a panic, having not been strong enough to force her hands from her throat. His defence was backed up by the doctor who had arranged to admit him in 1922 for further surgery on his arm, who said that Wood would have been incapable of gripping Miss White's throat in the manner described by the prosecution.

Mr Goodman Roberts, who had only recently been called to the Bar, did his best and told the jury that the first question to be solved was: had Miss White been killed at all or had she suffered a natural death? She had been in

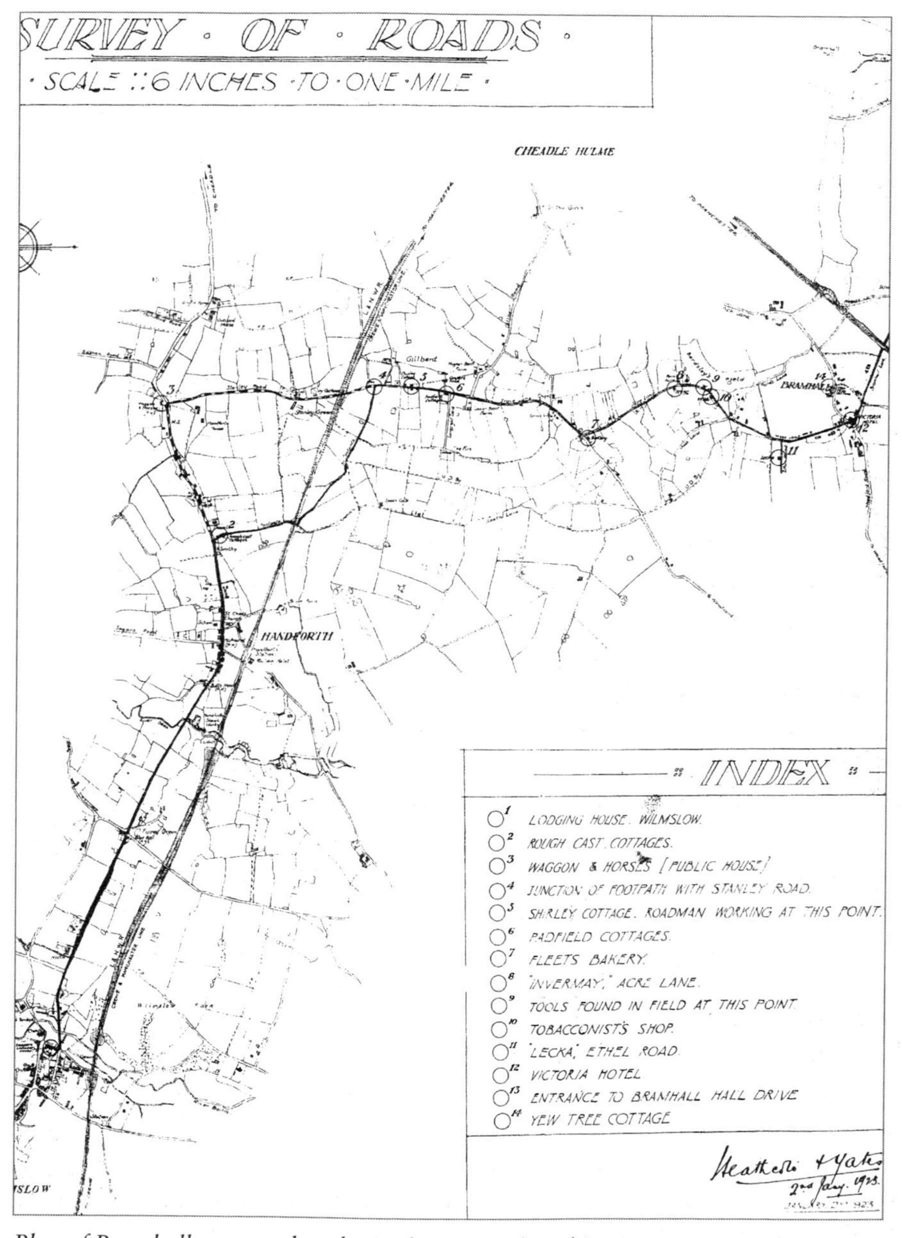

Plan of Bramhall area used at the trial. (National Archives)

indifferent health for some time and so could easily have had a seizure that morning and died from it. A possible theory, he tried to persuade the jury, was that Miss White had died from asphyxia because proper assistance had not been rendered to her at that moment; her head had not been held nor her clothing loosened. The prisoner might have seen this, and it was enough to strike terror into the heart of any man. If Miss White's hands had been tied before her death, why had she not screamed? Her next-door neighbour had deposed that she had heard the barking of the dog and hammering, so she should have been able to hear a scream.

Ellis Griffiths's address to the jury was confined to a résumé of the facts, pointing out that there was no evidence that Miss White had died from a stroke; if she had been strangled, then Wood must have been the murderer.

In his summing-up, Mr Justice Swift made mention of the lucid and closely reasoned manner in which Mr Goodman Roberts had conducted the case for the defence. Supposing the evidence of the prosecution's doctors to be correct, then somebody must have murdered Miss White; and though the jury had been asked by the defence to say that there was no motive for murder, the accused, while the lady had lain dead or dying, had thought it worthwhile to break open boxes and drawers. Did they know a greater motive for murder than cupidity, except cruel passion? He reminded the jury that the greed of gold had been the cause of numbers of people being done to death.

The jury then retired, returning late in the afternoon with a verdict of guilty, but with a strong recommendation to mercy. Wood stood silently in the dock, apparently unmoved. Asked by the Clerk of Assize if he had anything to say, the prisoner said, 'I still maintain that I am innocent, my Lord.' After assuring Wood that the jury's recommendation would be passed to the appropriate quarters, the judge donned the black cap and sentenced him to death. The prisoner then walked briskly out of the dock and was taken to the cells.

An appeal was heard on 26 March before the Lord Chief Justice, Lord Hewart of Bury, and Mr Justices Salter and Branson. The chief plank of the appeal was that the judge, in his summing-up, had told the jury that there was no question of anything but a verdict of murder, or acquittal. Wood's case was that Miss White had had a seizure and it was extraordinary that it had been suggested that the woman was throttled by the prisoner's left hand, which was practically useless. Without calling upon the prosecution, Lord Hewart reviewed the circumstances of the case and said that there was no substance whatever in the defence put forward. The appeal was dismissed.

The execution took place on 10 April 1923 at Walton Gaol, Liverpool. Unusually for the time, few people turned up to await the posting of the certificate of execution on the gaol's door, and by 7.45, only three men were outside, joined by a few labourers and two or three women as the clock ticked round to 8 a.m. John Ellis and Thomas Phillips officiated, the drop being 8ft 7in, and the governor confirmed that the execution had gone without a hitch.

11 THE CHINESE MYSTERY

Birkenhead, 1925

In the early part of the twentieth century, Price Street, Birkenhead, was the centre of a thriving Chinese community. Across the Mersey, in Liverpool, the Pitt Street area also contained many Chinese businesses, and the population of around 8,000 was the largest Chinese community outside London. The Navigation Act of 1850 stipulated that the crews of British ships had to be no less than 75 per cent British, but after repeal of the Act ship-owners were able to exploit the cheap labour that flooded in from the Orient, much of which settled in Liverpool.

Among the labourers was Lock Ah Tam, who arrived from Canton in 1895 as a ship's steward and eventually worked his way up to become the Liverpool representative of a firm of Hong Kong shipping-agents, becoming a naturalised Englishman along the way. Gradually, Lock Ah Tam had risen in the esteem of both Chinese and English nationals, and by the early 1900s he had become the European Representative of the Jack Ah Tia, an organisation of Chinese stevedores with headquarters in Hong Kong. He also rose to the rank of Superintendent of Chinese sailors for three British steamship companies. He took a particular interest in the well-being of the many hundreds of Chinese seamen who sailed in and out of Liverpool on a regular basis, and on occasion he dispensed informal justice to Chinese wrongdoers. Speaking good English, he was used by the government of the day to intercede in disputes affecting the local Chinese population and was generally regarded as something of a peacemaker. He was also well known for his charitable acts and for providing shoes and stockings for poor children

Lock Ah Tam. (Author's collection)

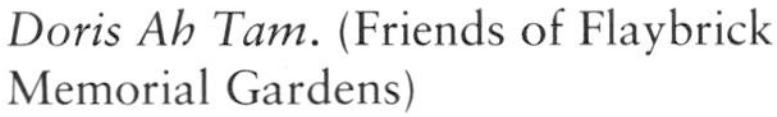

Doris Ah Tam. (Friends of Flaybrick Memorial Gardens)

Cecilia Ah Tam. (Friends of Flaybrick Memorial Gardens)

in his neighbourhood. Tam had founded a social club in Liverpool for Chinese seamen, which he named the Chinese Republic Progress Club, and he enjoyed shooting game, which he would often do with his English friend Percy Youd, who lived at 24 Westminster Road, Ellesmere Port. The two friends were also members of the Ellesmere Port Conservative Club.

In 1905, Tam met a Welsh girl in Cardiff, Catherine Morgan, and married her. Their first child, a son named Lock Ling Tam, was born in the same year, followed by David, who died at the age of 1 month; Doris, born in 1907; and a year later Cecilia, at which time the family moved to Birkenhead. Although they had an English mother and the girls had English first names, they took after their father in appearance, having pronounced oriental features.

Tam's business had prospered and he regularly held parties or celebrations at his home at 122 Price Street, a terraced three-storey property that had formerly been shop premises on the ground floor and from which he commuted each weekday to his business in Liverpool. On the evening of 11 August 1918, Tam decided to drop into the Republic Club before going home to his family, and he became involved in a brawl between some drunken Russian sailors. Suddenly, one of them picked up a billiard cue and dealt Tam a mighty blow on the back of the head, from which it took him more than a fortnight to recover.

In fact, it seemed to many that Tam never fully recovered from the blow, as little by little his friendly, peaceable character changed. He began to drink more, whereas before he had had only the occasional glass of whisky; became argumentative; and began to display sudden bursts of uncontrollable temper. His grip on the business slackened, and in 1924 he invested more than £10,000 (probably worth nearer a million at present-day prices) in a shipping venture which failed, losing Tam all his investment and causing his bankruptcy. The business was taken over by Kwok Tsan Chiu, a close friend of Tam, who lived next door at 120 Price Street. The telephone number at 122 was changed to Chiu's name and, to all outward appearances, he was now the owner of the business, although Tam continued to have ultimate charge. The bankruptcy severely affected him: he was much given to brooding about it and the considerable sum of money that he had lost.

It was one of the aspects of Chinese culture that people like Tam sent their first-born sons to China, often for several years, in order to learn the Chinese language and soak up some Chinese culture. These children often stayed with their paternal grandparents and many of them were not particularly enamoured at the prospect of leaving the place they regarded as home to travel to a faraway land with an alien language. Tam's son, Lock Ling, had been sent to Hong Kong in 1916, travelling to Canton in 1924 to attend the Christian College there, and it was his father's intention that he should stay until 1927. However, after being chosen to represent the Chinese Universities football team on their tour to New Zealand, Lock Ling returned to Hong Kong and travelled back to England in February 1925, ostensibly to assist his 55-year-old father with what remained of his business. However, Lock Ling was not particularly happy working for his father and preferred the motor trade, obtaining a job at the local Horsfall's Garage. He had a friend, a railway porter named Ah Foo (full name William

Drawing of front of 122 Price Street, Birkenhead. (National Archives)

Wing Ah Foo Cockbain), with whom he attended dances and theatres, but his father did not approve of the relationship and Ah Foo was seldom invited to Price Street. Instead the two friends usually met at Ah Foo's house at 2 Park Street, Birkenhead.

On 1 December 1925, Lock Ling Tam reached his majority according to the Chinese reckoning and his father proposed to hold a party for him at Price Street. Apart from Tam and his family, those attending included Ah Foo, Percy Youd, Mr and Mrs Chiu, Mr Frank Denye, with his wife and two sons, Margaret Sing (Mrs Tam's companion) and Mr and Mrs Clein.

After supper was over, the party continued with singing and dancing until about 12.45 a.m., when people started to drift away. According to Mr Denye, who had known Tam as a business acquaintance for about four years, everybody had appeared to be in good spirits. He had several conversations with Tam during the evening and he did not consider that his friend was suffering from the effects of drink.

Percy Youd later said that on the day of the party he had had a few drinks with Tam at the Westminster Hotel in Price Street and they returned to no. 122 at about 5.30 p.m. He was present at the party when Tam stood up to give the traditional toast to his son, saying, 'You are a man today. I hope that you will be as good a man as your father. I have given you a good education and am willing to spend more on your education if you require it, and I will do what I can for you.'

Mrs Tam then got up and said words to the same effect, after which Lock Ling replied to the toasts, saying 'Good health to all.' Percy Youd left the party at 9.45 p.m., his daughter having suffered an accident, and Tam told him before he left that if necessary he would send a car round if a doctor was needed. Youd described Tam as 'a kind and good friend – a real gentleman'.

The following events were described by Lock Ling Tam and others in their depositions, now with the National Archives.

The meal finished just before 10 p.m., at which time some champagne was drunk. Lock Ah Tam and Mr Denye also had whisky. By 12.45 a.m. on 2 December the party had broken up, Percy Youd and Ah Foo having left earlier. The party had gone well, with Tam dancing with his wife and everyone seeming perfectly happy, and the last ones to leave were the Denyes. At about 1 a.m. Lock Ling heard the sound of a quarrel coming from his father's bedroom. The sounds were loud enough to attract the attention of Doris and Cecilia, who joined their brother out on the landing. Then, together, they went into Tam's bedroom. Lock Ling believed that he had heard his mother exclaim in pain and demanded of his father that he should not hit his mother again. Tam appeared to be in a very bad temper and denied that he had hit his wife. Lock Ling then said, 'You are not going to hit her any more', and threatened to take her away, whereupon Tam said that if anyone were to go, it would be him (Tam). Tam then ordered everybody out of his room, including his wife, and they all stood on the landing for a short time before going into the sitting-room.

For reasons unknown, Lock Ling went next door to the Chius', where he stayed for about 10 minutes, and then, hearing screams coming from his own house, he and Mrs Chiu rushed out into the yard. Lock Ling found the scullery door locked against him, and after succeeding in breaking the kitchen window by throwing lumps of coal at it he climbed through into the kitchen and opened the door to admit Mrs Chiu. At that moment, his mother and sisters rushed down the stairs and joined them in the kitchen. Lock Ling pleaded with them to come out of the house, and while his sisters agreed, Mrs Tam was adamant that she would stay where she was, whereupon Lock Ling left the house again to look for a policeman. Failing to find one, he returned just in time to hear the sound of a shot. Looking through the broken kitchen window, he saw his father, who was now dressed in outdoor clothes, holding a revolver in his hand. Picking up a brass bowl that he had found in the yard, Lock Ling threw it at his father, but missed his target and ran off again to look for a policeman. As he ran, he heard a further three shots.

Margaret Sing, known as Maggie, was Mrs Tam's companion and had been employed as such for the past five years. She lived in at no. 122, sleeping in the same room as Doris and Cecilia, and had never had any reason to be unhappy with her lot. The family was a contented one and Lock Ah Tam had been good to her, although she had noticed that after the bankruptcy he had been prone to drink much more than he used to, usually whisky. When the first sounds of the quarrel arose the two daughters went downstairs, but Maggie stayed in bed, as she had been told by Tam on a previous occasion not to interfere with family affairs. After the two girls had been gone about 5 minutes, she heard Tam's voice calling to her, 'Go down in the parlour and bring my boots up.' She did as her employer asked, whereupon Tam told her to go upstairs and get dressed, which she did. Going back downstairs, she passed the half-open door of Tam's room and saw him, reflected in the mirror, carrying a revolver that she had often seen lying under the pillow when she made the beds. She also noticed two leather cases in the room, which she knew contained sporting guns. Quickly running into the sitting-room, she joined Mrs Tam and her daughters and told the frightened trio about the gun she had just seen. Now even more terrified, the women tried to barricade the door with furniture, and while they were doing this they heard Tam banging on the door, crying, 'Let me in!'

After a few minutes, everything went quiet and Mrs Tam opened the door slowly and looked out. Tam was nowhere to be seen, presumably having gone back into his bedroom, and the women took this opportunity to run downstairs into the kitchen, where they found Lock Ling and Mrs Chiu. After a short conversation, Lock Ling went out into the back yard and

Mrs Tam stood in the doorway leading from the kitchen into the scullery. Suddenly, Maggie Sing saw a gun pointing round the door into the scullery, although she could not see who was holding it. There was a report, and Mrs Tam fell backwards. Almost immediately, the gun turned to point at Cecilia. There was another report, and the girl slumped to the floor. Doris turned and said, 'Oh Maggie, isn't it awful? Daddy, what did you do that for?'

The kitchen door opened to disclose Lock Ah Tam, his face contorted with rage and froth around his lips. Raising the gun, he fired a further shot and Doris crumpled to the ground. Tam then turned on his heel and went upstairs. Without waiting to find out if any of the three women were still alive, Maggie ran out to the Chius' house and, not knowing where Lock Ling had gone, she and Mrs Chiu both went to find a policeman.

Shortly afterwards, Kwok Tsan Chiu, who up until then seems to have been content to let his wife investigate the situation on her own, went into the house and found Tam in his office. Speaking in Chinese, Tam said to his friend, 'I am in trouble. You look after the business and do your best. If I get hung, get my body out and bury me with my wife and daughters.' From this, it seems clear that Tam was fully aware of what he had done and the likely outcome of his actions. It would have been important to Tam to be buried with his family, in accordance with Chinese custom, although in the event this courtesy was to be denied him by the law.

At about 1.45 a.m., Lock Ah Tam telephoned the exchange and told telephonist John Edward Ellis, 'I have shot my wife and children. Please put me through to the town hall.' A startled Ellis connected him to the Borough Police Station, and Constable Robert Drysdale answered, 'Birkenhead Police speaking.' In reply, he heard a jumble of words, among which he recognised 'Tam', 'shot', 'killed', 'wife' and 'child'. The constable could tell that it was a foreign voice and, in reply to further questions, the voice continued, 'Send your folks please. I have killed my wife and child. My house is 122 Price Street.'

At about the same time, Lock Ling burst into the Birkenhead borough police station, begging Sergeant Arthur Thomas Hamer to come at once to his father's house. Pausing only to telephone the Central Police Office for reinforcements, Hamer accompanied Lock Ling back to Price Street, where he was joined by Sergeant Longford. Both front and back doors were now locked, so Longford climbed onto the yard wall and saw Lock Ah Tam in the back yard. To the policeman, he looked calm and collected and was able to speak quite rationally. There was no sign of any firearm.

'Will you please open the yard door', said Sergeant Longford, from his perch on top of the wall. 'Come round to the front', Tam replied, 'and I will let you in.' Hurrying round to the front of the house, they found Tam opening the door, saying quietly, 'Come in officers, I have done my wife in.' The two sergeants went into the house and Tam led the way into his office. Lighting a cigarette, Tam said, 'I have shot my wife.' Sergeant Hamer immediately cautioned the Chinaman, who continued, 'I shot my wife and daughters, they are in the back place.'

Catherine Ah Tam lay on her left side on the scullery floor, in a large pool of blood. Hamer bent down to touch the body, and judged that she was dead. Cecilia lay in another pool of blood, with her feet towards the yard door. She, too, appeared to be dead. Doris was in a sitting position immediately behind the door leading from the kitchen to the scullery. Switching on the light, Longford discovered that she was still breathing and he picked her up and laid her gently on the sofa. An ambulance was called, and Doris and the two dead women were removed to the hospital.

Returning to the office, Hamer questioned Tam more closely. 'I shot my wife with the gun in that case,' said Tam, pointing to a chair, on which rested a leather gun case containing a sporting gun and seventy-two cartridges, 'and I shot my daughters with revolvers.' When the sergeant asked where these guns were, Tam pointed to the safe and produced a bunch of keys from his pocket. When the safe was opened the policeman found a 5-chambered revolver, which contained 3 live cartridges, 1 spent cartridge case and 1 empty chamber. One of the live cartridges appeared to have been struck by the hammer of the pistol and had misfired. There was also an automatic pistol, although it was not clear whether this had been fired. Just then, Mrs Chiu came in and spoke to Tam in Chinese. Hamer promptly told her that she must not say anything to the prisoner, and if she wished to say anything at all it had to be in English. At about 2.25 a.m., Tam was taken to the Central Police Office, and on the way there, he said to Hamer, 'The trouble is through my son. My wife has not a kind word for me and my son is the cause of it.' Arriving at the police station, he was questioned by Superintendent Arthur Lodge, who, seeing that Tam was now in a very wild and agitated state, gave orders that he was not to be charged until he had calmed down. It was therefore 6.30 a.m. before he was charged by Sergeant Hamer with the murder of his wife. Tam replied, 'Nothing at present', giving a similar reply when further charges of murder in relation to the shooting of his daughters were made. Hamer noted that Tam now looked rational and perfectly sober, although there was a slight smell of drink about him, and he did not think it necessary to summon the police doctor.

Meanwhile, Dr James Bell Pettigrew Brown, Senior House Surgeon at Birkenhead Borough Hospital, had examined Catherine Ah Tam and her daughter Cecilia and pronounced them dead. At a post-mortem conducted later in the day, he found that Catherine had a deep lacerated wound over the region of the right collar bone and all the muscles of the right side of the neck, gullet and windpipe had been destroyed. Many small shot were found in the wound and the first to the fourth ribs on the right-hand side were broken in several places. There was no trace of powder around the wound, which indicated that the gun had been fired some way from the body.

Birkenhead Municipal Hospital, where the bodies of Mrs Ah Tam and Cecilia were first taken. (Friends of Flaybrick Memorial Gardens)

Cecilia had a wound in the side of her neck, extending deep into the body; passing through and behind the spine; and ending just under the skin of the back. There was some blackening, caused by particles of powder and small shot scattered throughout the wound.

In the hospital, Doris lay unconscious, breathing slowly. There was a bullet wound on the left side of her head about 3in above the ear, from which brain matter protruded, in addition to two more wounds above the left ear. The doctors thought that it was extremely unlikely that Doris would survive.

Lock Ah Tam was taken before the Birkenhead magistrates on 24 December and charged with two murders and one attempted murder, to which he reserved his defence. An inquest was adjourned to 27 January 1926. There, Maggie Sing told the coroner that her father was Chinese and her mother English, and that she had lived with the Tams for five years. She was unable to say whether anyone at the party had been drunk or not, but after she had gone to bed she had heard the sound of an argument coming from Tam's room. Being a little deaf, she was unable to say what the quarrel had been about and had not the slightest idea of what had caused it.

Lock Ling Tam agreed that he had thrown two lumps of coal, a piece of timber and a flower pot through the kitchen window and that he had swung a brass bowl at his father, but missed. He said that Tam had become very depressed after the bankruptcy, and that when he took a lot of whisky his father got 'strange ideas into his head'.

Sergeant Hamer gave evidence that he had known Tam for several years, and considered him an industrious man who had helped the police on many occasions.

The coroner then remanded Tam in custody, to await trial at Chester Assizes. On 25 December, John Woodend, Clerk to the Justices at Birkenhead, received a phone call summoning him to take a dying deposition from a person lying at the Borough Hospital. After serving the necessary legal notice on Lock Ah Tam, Woodend went to the hospital with Tam and Superintendent Lodge, also accompanied by Mr Frank Tweedle, JP and Dr Brown. When asked, Dr Brown stated that in his opinion Doris Ah Tam was not likely to recover from her injuries. He then informed Lock Ah Tam that they would endeavour to obtain from the semi-comatose girl a dying deposition as to how she came by her injuries. Mortally injured and in pain as she was, Doris was able to reply briefly to questions that were put to her, and the statutory deposition at the National Archives reads as follows:

> I live at 122 Price Street, Birkenhead. I went to bed last night, I don't know the time. I was awakened by hearing a noise. I heard a bullet. My father fired the bullet. I don't know who he fired it at. I did not see him fire at me. It was afterwards I saw my father. I heard the noise of the bullet. I don't know what happened then. I got out of bed when I was hit with the bullet. My neck hurt after the bullet. I heard my father shout to my mother. My father shot my sister before he shot me. He shot my mother. I saw him with a gun in his hand. He pointed it at my mother. I don't know whether my father pointed the gun at me.

The injured Doris was too ill to sign her name to the document, just managing to scrawl a cross. For a short time, she appeared to be making a recovery, and on 7 December Dr Brown operated on her, removing a piece of the left cheek bone, which was found to be broken off, and opening the wound in her skull in order to remove some pieces of bone from the brain. After she had been a week in hospital there was further improvement, and Brown removed a piece of bullet from her skull on 11 December. However, at the end of the first week in January 1926, a sudden change for the worse took place and Dr Brown discovered that an abscess had formed. Doris became rapidly worse and died at 8.50 p.m. on 21 January.

Tam's trial opened on Friday 5 February 1926 before Mr Justice McKinnon, with the charge now consisting of the murder of three persons. The Crown was represented by Sir Ellis Griffiths, and Tam by the redoubtable Sir Edward Marshall Hall. Hall was then coming to the end of his years at the Bar, after a splendid career as a defence advocate. He had for many years suffered badly from haemorrhoids, and his entrances into court were usually preceded by his junior carrying a small rubber ring upon which his master would sit in order to

Entrance to Crown Court, Chester Castle. (Cheshire County Council)

alleviate his condition. Hall, for this reason, was one of the very few advocates who were allowed to address the judge from a seated position. Junior counsel was John Grace, the President of the Ellesmere Conservative Club.

Tam was able to afford the fees of Marshall Hall because of subscriptions raised among the Chinese community throughout the length and breadth of the country, amounting to more than £1,000. Although Hall had been known to try all manner of theatrical tricks to rescue his clients from the gallows, he had little to work on in Tam's case, as there could be no doubt as to how the three women had died.

Sir Edward decided that the only way forward was to plead that when he had committed the murders Lock Ah Tam had been in a state of unconscious automatism, brought on by an epileptic fit. This, so he claimed, had been the result of the blow to the head that Tam had suffered several years before, which had made him subject to epilepsy. There was little chance of pleading insanity, as Tam had obviously known the exact position when he had rung the police and confessed to what he had done. In any case, the prosecution had the evidence of Dr J.M. Ahern, Medical Officer at Liverpool Prison, who certified that he was of the opinion that the prisoner, at the time of his crime, was not labouring under such a defect of reason from disease of the mind so as not to know the nature and quality of the act he was doing or to be incapable of knowing that what he was doing was wrong. In this, he was just following the words of the M'Naughton Rules, which laid down the terms under which a defendant might be considered to be insane. Ahern also declared that Tam was of sound mind and fit to plead.

Marshall Hall told the court that there was ample evidence that the Tam family had lived on the best of terms and that no sane man, after a happy family celebration and with no possible motive, could have perpetrated this terrible crime unless he had in some way been robbed of his senses. Backing up this plea was the evidence of Dr Ernest Reeve, a specialist in mental diseases, who confirmed Marshall Hall's theory of 'unconscious automatism' brought on by epilepsy, and aggravated by alcohol. Reeve attempted to persuade the court that in this state Tam would have been aware of everything that was going on around him at the time, but would later have had no recollection of what he had done. However, the Senior Medical Officer at Brixton Prison, Dr W.R.K. Watson, flatly denied that this was possible. He also backed up Dr Ahern's opinion that Tam was not insane under the terms of the M'Naughton Rules.

Hall did his best for Tam, insisting to the jury that no *sane* man could have done what Tam did. 'Are you not constrained to look for some explanation which is negative of sanity?' he cried to the jury; 'you are!' He then switched to the matter of Tam's ethnic origins, saying to the jury, 'I do not think we can get into the mind of an oriental and, fatalists as all orientals are, he must know that he must walk from this place to some place of detention . . . but

Crown Court, Chester Castle. (Mr Markwhite, Court Manager)

the nature of that place is of some moment to those who know him and were fond of him . . . It will be some consolation to them to feel that the man who was their friend, whom they loved, was safe. They would join in grateful thanks if you could say that though he was guilty of the act, he was insane at the time he did it.' Slumping into his seat, emotionally drained as he usually was after one of his perorations, Sir Edward Marshall Hall listened to the brief reply from prosecuting counsel and the judge's summing-up before the jury retired to consider their verdict. It took just 12 minutes for them to return a verdict of 'Guilty', surely a shamefully short time for twelve good men to have taken over such a verdict.

Tam showed no sign of concern for his fate, but he must have been heartened when he heard that his old friend Percy Youd had started a petition for his reprieve, which eventually contained almost 100,000 names.

At the appeal, which took place on 8 March 1926, just as the three judges were taking their seats those in court were astonished to see a dark-haired, clean-shaven young man wearing dark clothes and suede gloves rise from the back benches and proceed to give a long, rambling statement. Very little of this could be heard clearly, even by those sitting near him, although such phrases such as 'sent to prison twice', 'robbed by the Conservative Party' and 'I demand this right in the public interest' could be deciphered. At a sign from the Lord Chief Justice, several ushers appeared and forcibly ejected the man from the court.

Without wasting any further time, Tam's appeal against conviction was turned down, the Lord Chief Justice not even calling on Counsel for the Prosecution to be heard, and the revised date for execution was set as 23 March.

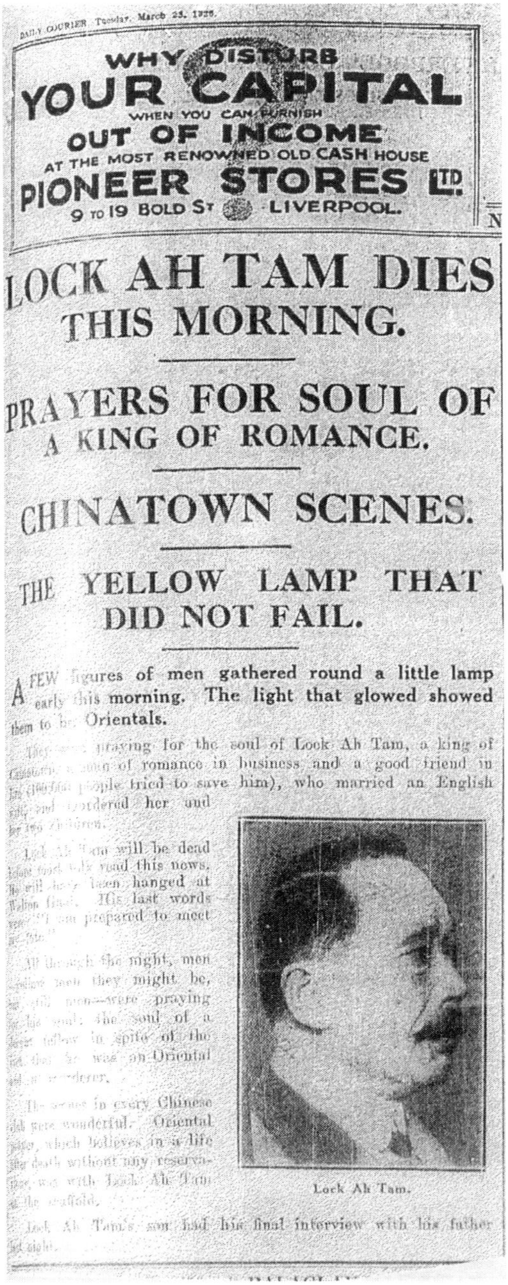
DAILY COURIER, Tuesday, March 23, 192[illegible]

WHY DISTURB YOUR CAPITAL WHEN YOU CAN FURNISH OUT OF INCOME AT THE MOST RENOWNED OLD CASH HOUSE PIONEER STORES LTD 9 TO 19 BOLD ST LIVERPOOL.

LOCK AH TAM DIES THIS MORNING.

PRAYERS FOR SOUL OF A KING OF ROMANCE.

CHINATOWN SCENES.

THE YELLOW LAMP THAT DID NOT FAIL.

A FEW figures of men gathered round a little lamp early this morning. The light that glowed showed them to be Orientals.

[illegible] praying for the soul of Look Ah Tam, a king of [illegible] of romance in business and a good friend in [illegible] people tried to save him), who married an English [illegible] murdered her and [illegible] children.

Lock Ah Tam will be dead [illegible] read this news. [illegible] been hanged at Walton [illegible]. His last words [illegible] "I am prepared to meet [illegible]."

All through the night, men [illegible] they might be, [illegible] men—were praying [illegible] soul: the soul of a [illegible] in spite of the [illegible] was an Oriental [illegible] murderer.

The scenes in every Chinese [illegible] were wonderful. Oriental [illegible], which believes in a life after death without any reservation, was with Look Ah Tam [illegible] the scaffold.

Lock Ah Tam's son had his final interview with his father last night.

Lock Ah Tam.

Extract, Cheshire Courier. (Cheshire Record Office)

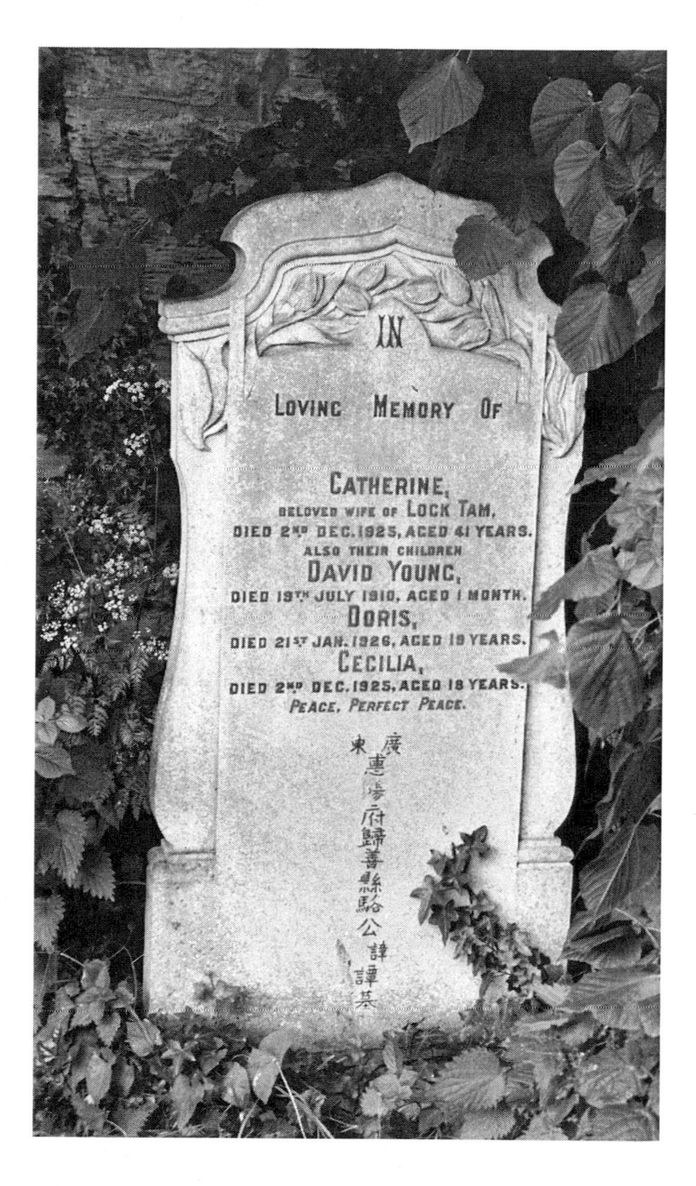

Grave of the Tam family at Flaybrick. (Author)

On 22 March, Percy Youd paid one final visit to his old friend, who thanked him for his efforts. 'Tell everyone that I shall meet my wife and daughters at 8 o'clock tomorrow morning. I believe in the Bible, I am not a heathen, although a Chinaman. You knew I loved my wife and daughters and if I had been in my right senses I would not shoot those I loved best, but the law is the law and I will go to my doom like a soldier, I shall not have to be helped to the scaffold.'

When the time allowed for visitors had expired, the two men shook hands and Youd said, 'Goodbye Tam, God bless you – the best Chinaman that ever lived, I shall always remember you.' Later the same day, Percy sent a telegram to Walton Gaol, voicing the same sentiments.

Catherine Ah Tam and her two daughters had been buried at Flaybrick Cemetery, 2 miles from Price Street, on 7 December. A procession of three horse-drawn hearses, each one loaded with floral tributes, had taken them on their last journey, in front of a large crowd lining the rain-soaked streets. It was Tam's last wish that he should be buried with them, as Chinese culture required, but this was not possible under Home Office regulations. On 23 March, Tam was hanged by William Willis and his body was buried within the precincts of Walton Gaol. The *Daily Courier* noted the event on its front page in large headlines – 'Lock Ah Tam dies this morning. Prayers for soul of a King of Romance. Chinatown Scenes.'

Today, a handsome headstone, carved with English and Chinese writing, still marks the grave of Catherine Ah Tam and her two daughters at Flaybrick. The Chinese characters read:

Guangdong Province
Hui Yang Prefecture
Guishan County
Luo*
Mr
Died
Tam
Tomb

Although Tam was not granted his wish to be buried with his wife and daughters, the inscription on the stone kept up the pretence and perhaps added some little comfort to his remaining family.

The real reason for this terrible tragedy will never be known. Marshall Hall's vain plea of temporary insanity consequent on the blow to Tam's head makes as much sense as anything, and it is perhaps only the enormity of the crime that made the Court of Appeal refuse a merciful reprieve.

*Luo was the nearest phonetical equivalent to 'Lock'.

12

A FARMHOUSE TRAGEDY

Alderley Edge, 1926

Finlow Farm, on the Mottram Road near Alderley Edge, an area famous for copper mines and wizards, was not a happy place. The farm was run by James Leah, a 60-year-old man with a reputation for having a violent temper. A large man, with a growth of thick, black beard tinted with grey, and a little too fond of the drink, he lived, on varying terms of goodwill, with his wife, daughters Elsie and Louise and son John. Quality furniture was definitely not a priority at Finlow Farm: in the back parlour a dresser reeled drunkenly on three legs, while much of the other furniture looked old, cracked and stained. There was no gas or electricity and a candlestick stood on a table, ready to light the way to bed.

Several of James's family farmed in the area, including his other daughter Margaret, now Mrs Jesse Leah, who had married the son of William Leah,

Exterior of Finlow Farm. (National Archives)

James's cousin. This had caused a rift in the family, as James, for some reason, had been against the marriage and refused to give his consent. Margaret, however, equally as fed up with her father as her mother and sisters appeared to be, ignored his protestations and married anyway; and for the next seven years, she avoided her father whenever she could. William Leah, her father-in-law, ran Dickins Farm, which was almost directly opposite Finlow Farm across Mottram Road. This meant that James Leah could not avoid meeting Jesse and his wife from time to time, but on those occasions he confined his conversation to a barely muttered passing of the time of day.

James Leah's moods worsened as his children grew up and began to seek a certain amount of independence, especially when Elsie and Louise reached the age when they became more interested in the lads from the village than they were in helping their mother around the farm. Things did not improve when his wife left the farm for a short time, taking Louise with her; and he was still smarting from when two years previously Louise had again decamped and obtained a job as a domestic servant in Wilmslow, although she had returned home again within the month.

John Leah had worked at Finlow Farm with his father since leaving school, but the old man's constant bad temper finally decided him to try and make a clean break, and on 11 September 1926, after warning his father two days before that if there weren't different goings-on he would leave, he was as good

Interior of Finlow Farm. (National Archives)

Site of gate of Finlow Farm, beyond which boyfriends did not venture. (Author)

as his word. James Leah protested and tried to persuade the boy to come back, but 20-year-old John had heard it all before and thought that his father was more concerned with the loss of a labourer than of a son. In addition, so frightened was he of his father's temper that he had chosen to sleep outside on more than one occasion in the past.

Elsie had a boyfriend, Frank Holland, who was well aware of James Leah's temperament, and in the two-and-a-half years that he and Elsie had been keeping company, he had never once been into the farmhouse. When the two came back from an evening out, Frank would leave Elsie at the farm gate on Mottram Road, leaving her to walk up the 200yd or so of cart track to the farmhouse on her own; although he had more than once passed the time of day with her father, he kept as much out of his way as he could.

On the evening of 23 September, Elsie and Frank left the farm at 6.45 p.m. and returned at about 8.20, pausing at the farm gate as usual. About 10 minutes later, James Leah got off the local bus and walked past them up the cart track to the house. He said nothing to them at that stage, but 10 minutes after he stormed down the field carrying a heavy stick and shouted at Frank Holland, 'I can't have this every night of the bloody week. You had all day yesterday and you've got to come again tonight!'

Fearing that if her father raised his voice any more he would be heard by passers-by on the road, Elsie tried to calm him down, saying, 'Don't carry on like that with people down the road. I won't be going out tomorrow night.'

This failed to mollify the angry farmer, who retorted that he didn't care who was down the road, or who heard him. He then took his coat off and threw it and the stick to the ground. Staring at Holland, he shouted, 'I don't need a stick!', and raised his fists in front of the young man's face. Holland realised that he would probably fare badly if it came to a fight with the inflamed farmer and followed Elsie's example, imploring the man to lower his voice so that passers-by would not be attracted to the scene. 'I don't care who knows,' replied Leah, although his voice was now lower. Turning on his heel, he made off towards the house, saying, 'I shan't speak again.'

With her father out of the way for the moment, Elsie kissed Frank goodnight and pushed him down the road. Once Holland was out of sight, she returned to the farmhouse where her mother and father were sitting in the parlour. Leah looked at her and growled, 'I wished I had given him a bit more,' and then, his voice rising rapidly, 'If he is there again tomorrow night and the other bugger [meaning Louise's young man] I'll finish them off!' These threats against his daughters' boyfriends had been growing ever more frequent, but this time Elsie, used to her father's tantrums and perhaps realising that the time was rapidly approaching when Frank would pop the question and take her away from all this unpleasantness, dug in her heels. 'You won't have a chance', she told her father, 'because I'll go in the morning.'

At 9.45 p.m., James Leah went up to bed, leaving his wife and daughters talking among themselves. Perhaps stiffened by Elsie's show of courage, the three women discussed the events of the evening in low voices and, before long, mother and daughters had decided that they would all leave on the following morning, this time for good. With that thought in their minds, they went up to their respective beds.

The next morning, 24 September, a breakfast was prepared which they all ate without exchanging a word. James must have realised that something was up, but put his coat on and went out down the track with the horse and cart. At 10 a.m., his wife and her younger daughter left the house, taking with them as much of their belongings as they could manage. Somewhat to Elsie's surprise Louise returned within a short time, but volunteered no information as to why she had done so. The two girls were preparing some food for themselves when James came in, seeming very annoyed that their mother had left, 'but not much upset', thought Elsie, who had arranged for a taxi to call in the afternoon to take her and her sister, and the rest of their belongings, away. Suddenly, James burst out, 'Where has your mother gone?' 'You ought to know where she has gone,' Elsie retorted. James glowered. 'It's been a planned job,' he snarled, and stormed out of the house. For the next hour or so, he came in and out restlessly and at one time followed Elsie into the milkhouse. 'When are you going?' he asked angrily. 'Today,' she replied and continued with her work, trying her best to ignore her father and the strained atmosphere that he had created. At about 11.30 a.m., Elsie left to get a taxi,

Mottram Road, showing entrances to both farms. (Author)

leaving Louise alone with her father. 'I shan't be long,' she shouted to her sister as she left; 'I will get back as soon as I can.'

At about noon, William Salter, a roadman working for Macclesfield RDC on the Mottram Road, went into the stable at Dickins Farm to eat his lunch. Earlier in the morning, he had seen James Leah coming from the direction of Alderley Edge with the horse and cart, but now, suddenly, he saw a young woman he did not know stumbling towards the back kitchen door of the farmhouse. She was covered in blood and bleeding profusely from wounds in the head and neck. According to Salter's evidence at the trial, she was 'rather staggerified', and without waiting to see if he could give any help he set off on his bicycle to find an ambulance.

William Leah and his daughter-in-law Margaret were both in the back kitchen when the badly injured Louise staggered into the house. The horrified Margaret rushed to take her sister in her arms but was pushed aside by Louise, who slumped into a rocking-chair near the fire, obviously in a bad way. Hastily, they laid the girl down on the floor and tried desperately to staunch the stream of blood coming from her head, while William shouted orders to one of his farm-hands to fetch a doctor as quickly as possible. Dr Buchanan, from Alderley Edge, arrived and found Louise lying on the kitchen floor semi-conscious, soaked in blood down to her underclothing.

Blood was still flowing, and in addition to the cuts to her head and neck she had gashes on the second and third fingers of her right hand, just over the middle joint, cut to the bone. The laceration at the back of her neck was clearly very deep, having severed all the muscles and reached to the spine, exposing the spinal cord. It was a miracle that the girl had walked all the way from her home to Dickins Farm without collapsing. While the doctor was attending to her the injured girl attempted to say something to him, but the effort was too much and she lapsed into unconsciousness. Dr Buchanan, with the assistance of Dr Baker, who had also been summoned, made Louise as comfortable as possible and assisted in taking her to the local cottage hospital, accompanied by her sister Elsie, where she died in the late afternoon.

Meanwhile, the police had been called to Finlow Farm, and Sergeant Stephen Barber and Constable George Wakelow arrived at about 2.30 p.m. to search the premises. On the left, as they entered the farm, they saw a large black wooden shed, about 15ft long. The door was closed but not locked, and inside, lying on the floor, they found a hedge knife stained with blood and with a quantity of hair sticking to it. A pile of potatoes also had blood on it, as had some sacks. Going into the kitchen, they found more bloodstains on the dresser, 3ft long and 8in wide, and more bloodspots on the floor, with a pool of blood extending 10ft across the back of the kitchen. A meal appeared to have been laid for four people, and two of the cups had been used recently.

A trail of blood led from the house and extended along a pathway to a stile leading to the wood, where there was a break in the rail fence and Wakelow noticed a small piece of bloodsoaked material on the ground. Nearby was a fodder bin, which Barber examined closely. It appeared to be full of hay, but suddenly there was a movement and the policeman found to his surprise that underneath the hay was James Leah, lying in concealment. The front of his clothing was saturated with blood and he was bleeding from a wound under his throat.

Recognising the policeman, Leah called out, 'Oh Mr Barber, my poor daughter.' Barber cautioned him, in reply to which Leah said, 'She is the best girl I have got and I could not bear for her to go.' Leah was searched and a bloodstained penknife was taken from him, after which he was taken to the cottage hospital for his wounds to be treated. It was there that he made a statement: 'I did her in in the back kitchen, then I cut myself with the hedge knife and went to the fodder bin to finish myself off with the penknife. She's the best girl I've got – poor Louise.'

The post-mortem on the dead girl was carried out the following day by Dr Buchanan, assisted by Dr Macassock. They reported that the wounds on the dead girl's right-hand side were roughly an inch long, penetrating to the bone, and had been caused in her attempt to fight off her father's assault with the hedge knife. On the scalp, the wound on the right side above the ear was a large lacerated scalp wound about 2in by 1½in wide, also penetrating to the bone. A second wound behind the left ear was 3in long, gaping ½in, and it was probably this wound that had proved fatal.

Leah was remanded in custody at Wilmslow Sessions House to await trial, and the *Chester Chronicle* of 2 October 1926 reported that, when charged, Leah said that he was no scholar and would have to get someone to speak for him. Later, while still in gaol, he sent for Sergeant Barber. 'I remember you telling me something, Sergeant, and I have been thinking about it. Has there been a death?' It would seem at this stage that James Leah was trying to deny all knowledge of his crime, as he had been clearly charged with the murder of his daughter when arrested and had had plenty of time to think about it in the meantime. 'Louise is dead,' Barber told him, at which the accused man broke down in tears. 'I would rather have been parted with anyone other than that girl,' he sobbed, and after that refused to see any of his family before the trial.

On Wednesday 27 October, Mr Justice Fraser presided at Chester Castle, with Mr Dallas Walters appearing for the defence. From the evidence, it was clear to the court that Leah was a man who burnt on a short fuse and could fly into a temper at the slightest provocation. Neither his wife nor his children could bear him and all, at one time or another, had left the farm for short periods. James Leah's quarrelling with the boyfriends of two of his daughters was brought out, in particular the fact that he had made it quite clear to them that they were not welcome on his property. Frank Holland told the court that he was sure that Leah was jealous of him and thought, probably rightly, that he was trying to steal Elsie's affections from him. Margaret Leah was of the same opinion so far as her own case was concerned.

The medical evidence showed that Louise's wounds had been caused by the hedge knife found in the house and that her father's wounds were self-inflicted with the penknife found in his possession.

Dallas Walters had a difficult task in defending Leah. The main facts were proved, and it was clear that Leah had killed his daughter before making a half-hearted attempt to commit suicide. Walters suggested to the court that his client had had no time to form intent, as the attack had been committed on the spur of the moment. Leah had pleaded with Louise to stay after she had told him that she intended to leave, but she had only answered him 'snappily'. Leah cut a poor figure in the witness box and protested that he had had no intention of causing Louise any grievous bodily harm. 'I was that weighed down with trouble because her mother and all had gone', he sobbed.

Mr Williams, Agent to Lord Stanley of Alderley, the local landowner, reported that Leah was an abnormal man, who laboured under delusions. However, Dr Ahern, Senior Medical Officer at Liverpool (Walton) Prison, told the court that he could not find any evidence of mental disease in the accused, although there were signs of emotional weakness: 'I would say that he would be subject to outbursts of emotional excitement which would often take the form of anger. During the first stages of these outbursts of excitement, he would not be fully conscious of the results of his actions, or of the purpose he had in view. After a short time, realisation of what he had done would come to him and he would be filled with remorse.' Despite repeating, under further questioning from the prosecution, that Leah showed no signs of mental disease, Dr Ahern had, in fact, just indicated to the court that Leah had exhibited some, if not all, of the requirements of the M'Naughton Rules as regards the possibility of his being insane at the time of the crime. The Rules, which for many years had formed the basis of any insanity plea, required the defence to show that the accused was labouring under such disease of the mind that he did not know what he was doing, or that if he did know, he did not know that it was wrong.

Ahern had just told the court exactly that, and had then turned his evidence on its head by insisting that Leah showed no signs of mental illness. It is clear that defence counsel should have pressed this point much more than he did and that Leah's defence suffered because of it.

During the judge's summing-up, which occupied a considerable time, the accused sat quietly in the dock, his head sunk onto his chest. The jury, consisting of ten men and two women, retired to consider their verdict at 6.48 p.m. and returned exactly 1 hour later with a verdict of guilty, with a recommendation to mercy. While James Leah gazed at him fixedly, Mr Justice Fraser pronounced the death sentence, and said that he would see that the recommendation was forwarded to the proper quarter.

An appeal was turned down on 12 November and Colonel Rich, Governor of Walton Gaol, signed the standard letter to the Home Secretary, asking for a list of candidates reported to be competent for the office of executioner and a copy of the memorandum of instructions for carrying out the details of an execution, plus a copy of the table of drops. In reply, the Commissioners desired him to satisfy himself personally that the instructions were carefully and promptly carried out in every detail, adding that 'if an assistant executioner is required, Mann is recommended'.

The *Liverpool Echo* reported that the execution took place at 8 a.m. on Tuesday 16 November at Walton Gaol, Liverpool. There were only about a score of people outside the prison to await the notice of execution and the small crowd stood in silent groups until 8 a.m. struck on a neighbouring clock, when several raised their hats for a second or two. The *Cheshire Chronicle* noted that the execution, carried out by Thomas Pierrepoint, assisted by Lionel Mann, was performed skilfully and decorously, the drop being 6ft 8in, resulting in instantaneous death.

The poor, quick-tempered farmer, a human time-bomb waiting to go off, who had almost certainly killed under extreme emotion and, as the prison doctor had admitted, had probably not known what he was doing at the time of the actual deed, was now at peace, although a little more application by his defence counsel might well have saved him from the gallows.

13

DEATH ACROSS THE DEE

Chester, 1928

Greenway Street, in the Handbridge district of Chester, has changed over the past eighty years, many of the houses having been demolished and rebuilt. Even so, the street is still cobbled as it drops down steeply to the banks of the River Dee. Looming high above the opposite bank of the river is the grim façade of Chester Castle, scene of many trials and executions. Halfway down the right-hand side of the street, the road drops sharply below pavement level, forming a small wall known to the locals as 'the parapet'.

In November 1927, William Dobson, a 28-year-old fisherman, married and with two children, lived at 7 Greenway Street, while his working partner John James White lived at no. 9. It was a close community, and John White's aunt, Mrs Hannah White, lived near him at no. 35. On 11 November 1927, Dobson and White were working their small boat, net fishing on the River Dee, when a storm blew up. Young White got tangled in the nets, fell overboard and, despite Dobson's best efforts, was swept away by the current and drowned. His body was found the following day on the banks of the river at Connahs Quay, about 7 miles from where the accident happened, and it was said that Dobson, who was generally thought by everyone to be a respectable and likeable young man, was stricken by the untimely death of his friend and tended thereafter to be of a mournful disposition.

Greenway Street, showing 'the parapet'. (Author)

CERTIFIED COPY OF AN ENTRY OF DEATH
COPI DILYS O GOFNOD MARWOLAETH

Given at the GENERAL REGISTER OFFICE
Fe'i rhoddwyd yn y GENERAL REGISTER OFFICE

Application Number / Rhif y cais: COL818144

REGISTRATION DISTRICT / DOSBARTH COFRESTRU: Holywell

1927 DEATH in the Sub district of / MARWOLAETH yn Is-ddosbarth: Flint in the / yn County of Flint

Columns: Colofnau:	1	2	3	4	5	6	7	8	9
No. / Rhif	When and where died / Pryd a lle y bu farw	Name and surname / Enw a chyfenw	Sex / Rhyw	Age / Oed	Occupation / Gwaith	Cause of death / Achos marwolaeth	Signature, description and residence of informant / Llofnod, disgrifiad a chyfeiriad yr hysbysydd	When registered / Pryd y cofrestrwyd	Signature of registrar / Llofnod y cofrestrydd
445	Twelfth November 1927 On the Banks of the River Dee at [illegible] in the Parish of Connah's Quay U.D.	John James White	Male	23 years	Fisherman of No 9 River View Greenway Street Handbridge in the City of Chester	Found drowned the deceased being accidentally drowned on the 7th day of November 1927 by falling from a Boat from which he was fishing into the River Dee No P.M.	Certificate received from Fred Llewellyn-Jones Coroner for the County of Flint Inquest held 14th November 1927	Seventeenth November 1927	J. W. Conway Deputy Registrar.

CERTIFIED to be a true copy of an entry in the certified copy of a Register of Deaths in the District above mentioned.
TYSTIOLAETHWYD ei fod yn gopi cywir o gofnod mewn copi y tystiwyd iddo o Gofrestr Marwolaethau yn y Dosbarth a enwyd uchod.

See note
Gweler

Given at the GENERAL REGISTER OFFICE, under the Seal of the said Office,
Fe'i rhoddwyd yn y GENERAL REGISTER OFFICE, o dan Sêl y swyddfa a enwyd,

the / y 14th day of / dydd o fis July 2005

CAUTION: THERE ARE OFFENCES RELATING TO FALSIFYING OR ALTERING A CERTIFICATE AND USING OR POSSESSING A FALSE CERTIFICATE. © CROWN COPYRIGHT
GOFAL: MAE YNA DROSEDDAU YN YMWNEUD Â FFUGIO NEU ADDASU TYSTYSGRIF NEU DDEFNYDDIO TYSTYSGRIF FFUG NEU WRTH FOD AG UN YN EICH MEDDIANT. © HAWLFRAINT Y GORON

WARNING: A CERTIFICATE IS NOT EVIDENCE OF IDENTITY.
RHYBUDD: NID YW TYSTYSGRIF YN PROFI PWY YDYCH CHI.

WDXZ 070800

027247 7286 04/04 SPSL 007708

LBH

Death certificate of John White. (Crown Copyright)

This unfortunate accident, for the inquest placed no blame on William Dobson, also took its toll on Hannah White, who, it has to be said, was rather fonder of the bottle than she should have been. Hannah was only about 5ft 5in tall, but weighed in the region of 12 stones; and lately, when she was in her cups (a frequent occurrence), she had acquired a habit of shouting to whoever would hear her that Dobson was guilty of the wilful murder of her beloved nephew and that something should be done about it. She had served a one-month prison sentence for assault and had over forty previous convictions, mostly connected with drink. Her neighbours were well aware of Hannah's shortcomings and bore her rantings with fortitude, though at the same time they wondered to themselves at the forbearance of William Dobson, who studiously ignored the severe provocation that his neighbour obviously gave him.

On the night of 7 April 1928, Hannah was even more vociferous than usual, with a constant stream of profanities and accusations pouring from her drunken lips. She could be heard all over Greenway Street, and even her hardened neighbours were beginning to tire of her continual ravings. Earlier in the evening, she had waged a verbal battle with another neighbour, Mr Buckley, and later began a tirade against Dobson. 'The ship that never returned,' she warbled at the top of her voice; 'but you, you bloody pig, you returned, but John James never returned. You drowned him, you know you drowned him, Billy Dobson.'

At about 9.45 p.m., William returned home from his day's work, exhausted from his labours and no doubt wishing for nothing more than his dinner and a pipeful of tobacco by the kitchen range. However, he was not to be granted this boon, for he was accosted by a neighbour and acquainted with the events

Greenway Street from across the River Dee. (Author)

earlier that evening. In his hungry and weary state Dobson decided that enough was enough, and he stormed down Greenway Street to no. 35, where Hannah was still up to her antics.

Meanwhile, across the River Dee, at about 10 p.m., Detective Inspector William Stockton of the railway police was walking along Castle Drive, which runs parallel to the river. As he reached a point immediately opposite Greenway Street, he heard someone shouting. 'Looking across', he said later, 'I saw it was a woman. I could see quite clearly, the street was illuminated and the woman was staggering about in the roadway at the time.' Half an hour later, when returning from the opposite direction, he again paused as he came level with Greenway Street and saw the same woman, who was still shouting. 'The next thing I saw was a man coming down the street and coming past the street lamp. I saw the man walk down the footpath towards the bottom of the street and, at the same time, the woman staggered up to the edge of the footpath and they appeared to meet at right angles. Immediately they met, I saw the man raise his arm and strike the woman – she fell to the ground and I heard a dull thud, as though it was her head striking the ground. There was a dog barking furiously at the time, as though it was attacking someone. I heard two more blows, which sounded more like the noise from a belt being used. Then the man walked up the street beyond the lamp, and I saw that he was not wearing a jacket or a waistcoat. I could not see whether the man had anything in his hand or not. The woman was using bad language.'

Detective Inspector Stockton's vantage point to the scene of the disturbance was about 75yd, and although he claimed that it was a 'fairly clear night', the moon was not visible and Greenway Street was lit only by two street lamps, each containing the equivalent of a 60-watt bulb. Edwin Ashley, who lived at no. 23, was later to tell the police that the street was dark and he was not able to see very well when he went out, making Stockton's feats of vision and hearing somewhat remarkable. Ashley went on to say that he had heard shouting from the street and, on opening his front door, had seen Dobson bending over the fallen shape of Hannah White and shouting, 'I have bloody well done her in! I don't care if I bloody well hang for her!' The man was wearing neither coat nor waistcoat, and was carrying what appeared to be a hammer over his left shoulder. Straightening up, Dobson walked quickly towards his own front door, and as he passed no. 21 he growled to Florence White, 'I've bloody well done it now. You can go and see her.'

Thomas Johnson, a fisherman who lived at no. 29, gave evidence at the trial that he, too, had heard the shouting and the barking of a dog and, on going outside, he had found Mrs White on the pavement, her head in the gutter. 'I lifted her head up', he said, 'and it was soft and bleeding.' By that time, the night was quite dark and it was raining slightly. He bathed the woman's face with water, and saw that she was still breathing heavily. Later, he helped to carry her body into the house, assisted by two of his neighbours. He said also that the dog was running round the body, barking furiously and appearing very vicious.

The fracas had by now been brought to the attention of the police, and during the latter part of the evening Chief Inspector Griffiths interviewed Robert Buckley, who had been arguing with Hannah White earlier in the evening. Buckley was taken to the police station where he was detained, pending further enquiries, but was later released without charge. It was 2 a.m. on Sunday before Griffiths knocked on the door of no. 7, where he was admitted by Mrs Dobson and shown into the front parlour. After a long discussion with her husband, the inspector cautioned him and placed him under arrest. A statement, written hastily in pencil, now at the National Archives, read:

> William Dobson, 29 years, states, I was cautioned by DI Griffiths that he was making enquiries respecting the death of Mrs Hannah White of 35 Greenway Street. About 10.10, I was coming down the lane at Greenway Street to my home, no. 7, when I heard Hannah White shouting. My wife told me that Hannah was saying that I had drowned her nephew. It preyed on my mind and I went down the lane and saw her standing just off the parapet. I asked what she was saying about me. I shoved her a-one-side and hit her with my fist. I shouted she will not get up any more. That's the lot. This statement I make of my own free will, signed William Dobson and witnessed by Hannah Dobson, James Griffiths and Pennant Lloyd (Sergeant).

A desultory search of the house found nothing, but when Griffiths returned later on the following day he found a large hammer. This object, in Griffiths's words, 'looked as though it had been carefully washed, in other words it was wet'. On being questioned, the inspector thought that the hammer had been wiped 2 or 3 minutes before he arrived, although what evidence there was for this astounding statement was never made clear. He then examined the shirt that Dobson was said to have been wearing earlier that evening, but could find no blood on it.

Dr W.H. Grace MD, Pathologist at Chester Royal Infirmary, conducted the post-mortem on Sunday 8 April and his report, dated 10 April, states that with the exception of the injuries to the skull there was no disease in any of the organs sufficient to account for death. There was a considerable amount of clotted blood in the woman's hair and there was fresh blood issuing from her left ear. There was a deep incised wound 2in long over the right eye and another similar wound above this, at the base of the hair. Her right cheek was bruised, and at the back of the head, over the occipital bone, there was a ragged circular wound about 3in in diameter. Removal of the scalp disclosed two skull fractures, and a circular piece of bone of 2½in diameter had been driven into the skull and was lying on the brain. Cause of death was shock due to compound fracture of the posterior wall and a simple fracture to the base of the skull.

The trial began at Chester Assizes before Mr Justice Shearman on Wednesday 20 June, with Artemus Jones QC and J.P. Elsden appearing for Dobson, while the prosecution lay in the hands of Lord Halsbury KC, assisted by Stanley Davis.

Halsbury, in an eminently fair résumé of the case, pointed out to the jury that Dobson was a man of hitherto unblemished character who had been sorely provoked by the constant mutterings of the deceased and her none-too-subtle hints that he had been responsible for the death of her nephew. 'The accusation', he told the jury, 'is as cruel as it is unfounded.' He would not dispute that allegations had been made on many occasions and that they amounted to a serious provocation, but that did not excuse murder, and murder it undoubtedly was. Halsbury's suggestion was that when Hannah White was knocked to the ground, Dobson had deliberately taken a hammer and smashed her skull in; although he stopped short of saying that if Dobson had carried a hammer on that fatal evening, the act must have been premeditated.

Dr Grace caused some alarm in the courtroom when he produced Hannah White's skull to demonstrate how the hammerhead fitted the depression almost exactly. He showed that the dead woman's skull was thicker than normal, and so the second fracture would have required a very heavy blow to cause it.

Dobson's sister, Mrs Mary Jane Davies, was called to the witness box, but collapsed before she could get there and was carried from the court. William Dobson then told the court that he had enlisted in the army at the age of 16 and had served thoughout the First World War. In reply to questions from Artemus Jones, he denied that he had used a hammer to strike Hannah White, but did admit that he had been very angry when he had confronted her. He also claimed, in answer to a question by Halsbury, not to have realised that Hannah White was dead when he had left her on the ground.

The defence then began a half-hearted attempt to prove that Dobson had been insane when he had struck the blows, but the learned judge would have none of it. Dr Hamilton Grills, Medical Superintendent of the Cheshire County Mental Hospital, was put firmly in his place when he attempted to suggest that the provocation that Dobson had undergone could have turned his mind.

That closed the case for the defence, and Lord Halsbury, who throughout the trial had bent over backwards to be fair to the accused, announced that although he had the right of last word (as Dobson had called witnesses), he was of a mind to waive it. He therefore addressed the jury first, describing Dobson walking back to his house and putting his arms around his wife, saying, 'Oh Mum, what have I done?' Dobson himself had admitted that he had been mad with anger and Halsbury told the jury that he had no doubt that this had been the case. 'It was too much for him,' said the lawyer; 'he goes out not only with the idea of knocking her down, but with the deliberate idea of killing her.' If these facts were right, it would be the jury's duty, whatever sympathy they felt for the accused, to return a verdict of guilty of murder.

Memorial to George Marsh, Protestant Martyr, at Boughton, Chester, site of the public gallows. (Author)

In an eloquent speech, Artemus Jones submitted that the evidence before the jury did not entitle them to return a verdict of guilty of murder. None of the witnesses had said that they had seen any hammer blow struck; and if the hammer had been washed 2 or 3 minutes before Inspector Griffiths had found it on the Sunday, it could not have been washed by Dobson, who was by then in custody. He made a strong plea for a verdict of manslaughter.

The judge, summing up, said that it was in the power of the jury to reduce the charge to manslaughter, but only if the provocation was sufficient to deprive a reasonable man of his self-control. If they found a verdict of guilty of murder it was open to them to add a recommendation to mercy, although it did not necessarily follow that it would have the desired effect. The jury retired at 4.55 p.m., returning 35 minutes later with a verdict of guilty of murder, with a strong recommendation to mercy. Dobson took the verdict and the subsequent death sentence without a word, and afterwards walked calmly to the cells below.

Within a few days a committee for the defence of William Dobson had been formed, consisting of members of Chester City Council and the Board of Guardians. By 14 July, the petition for a reprieve bore about 9,000 signatures, over 1,000 forms having been circulated in the Chester area.

The appeal was heard on Monday 16 July 1928 by Lord Hewart, the Lord Chief Justice, sitting with Justices Acton and Branson. Artemus Jones told their lordships that the appeal was on the ground that Mr Justice Shearman had not put to the jury either adequately or satisfactorily what the defence actually comprised. The witness Stockton had seen the tragedy from the other side of the river, which was about 30yd wide at that point and although he had said he had a clear view, other witnesses had said

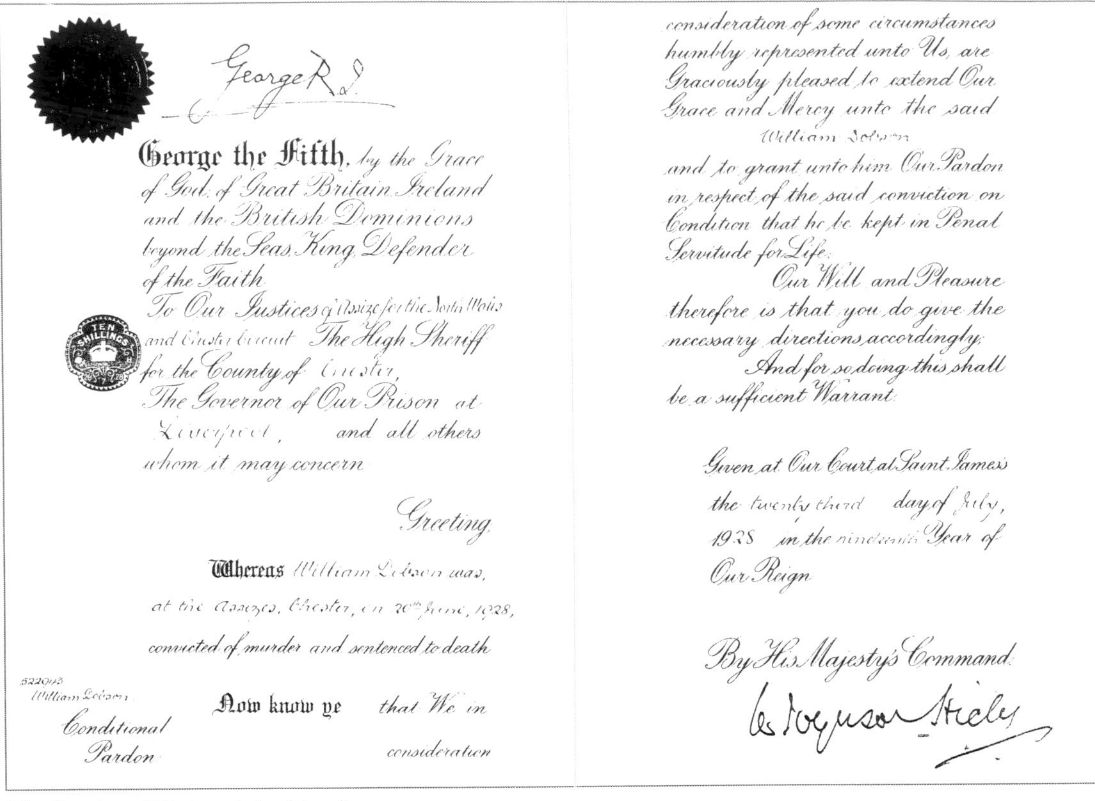

George R.I.

George the Fifth, by the Grace of God, of Great Britain Ireland and the British Dominions beyond the Seas King, Defender of the Faith

To Our Justices of Assize for the North Wales and Chester Circuit The High Sheriff for the County of Chester, The Governor of Our Prison at Liverpool, and all others whom it may concern

Greeting

Whereas William Dobson was, at the Assizes, Chester, on 20th June, 1928, convicted of murder and sentenced to death

Now know ye that We in consideration of some circumstances humbly represented unto Us, are Graciously pleased to extend Our Grace and Mercy unto the said William Dobson and to grant unto him Our Pardon in respect of the said conviction on Condition that he be kept in Penal Servitude for Life.

Our Will and Pleasure therefore is that you do give the necessary directions accordingly.

And for so doing this shall be a sufficient Warrant.

Given at Our Court at Saint James's the twenty third day of July, 1928 in the nineteenth Year of Our Reign.

By His Majesty's Command

W Joynson-Hicks

522043
William Dobson
Conditional Pardon

The Pardon. (National Archives)

that it was dark. Mrs White had been struck two blows with a fist and had fallen backwards, hitting her head on the pavement; and it was this that had caused the injuries to the skull. As for the hammer, Dobson's father said that he kept a ferret in a cage above the place where it had been found, and the dampness could well have been caused by his sluicing out the cage. The learned judge had also mentioned to the jury that Mrs White had very thick hair that could well have shielded Dobson from any of her blood. No evidence had been introduced on this very important point; and it was just something in the judge's mind. It was a vital point for the defence that no blood had been found on Dobson's clothes.

Without troubling himself with anything from Lord Halsbury, the Lord Chief Justice dismissed the appeal and said that it was clear that Dobson had armed himself with a hammer and gone out for the purpose, at any rate, of inflicting grievous bodily harm on Hannah White.

A week before the execution was due to take place, word came from the Home Office that the sentence had been reduced to life imprisonment. Dobson subsequently served a relatively lenient seven years, before being released in August 1935 to sink into anonymity.

At the time of the trial, some people may have remembered that Mr Artemus Jones QC had been in the limelight himself eighteen years before, when he was personally involved in a notorious libel case. The *Sunday Chronicle* had published a fictional story in 1910, a section of which read:

> There is Artemus Jones with a woman who is not his wife, who must be, you know, the other thing,' whispered a fair neighbour of mine excitedly into her bosom-friend's ear.

The character Jones was said to be a churchwarden from Peckham and the allegation was clearly that he was an adulterer. This was pointed out to the real Artemus Jones, with some glee, by two of his friends. He sued for libel and won the not inconsiderable sum in those days of £1,700 in damages, after the case had gone to the House of Lords.

BIBLIOGRAPHY

ABBREVIATIONS

PRO – Public Record Office (now the National Archives)

1. THE CONGLETON CANNIBAL

Head, Robert, *Congleton Past & Present*, 1887
Lee, Sarah, *Classic Murders of the North West*, Forum Design, 1999
Pearson, Jeffrey, *Cheshire Tales of Mystery & Murder*, Countryside Books, 2002
Yarwood, Derek, *Outrages – Fatal and Other*, Didsbury Press, 1991
Congleton Chronicle – Almanac & Guide, 1897
Chester Courant
Manchester Mercury

2. DEATH IN THE DINGLE

Bailey, Brian, *Hangmen of England*, Allen, 1989
Pearson, Jeffrey, *Cheshire Tales of Mystery & Murder*, Countryside Books, 2002
Yarwood, Derek, *Outrages – Fatal and Other*, Didsbury Press, 1991
Notable British Trials series: *George Chapman*, Adam, H.L. (ed.), Hodge, 1930

3. MURDER MISTAKEN?

Staffordshire Advertiser, July 1835
Family History Society of Cheshire – Crewe Group website:
http://www.scfhs.org.uk/scfhs/mary_malpas.html

4. DOUBLE MURDER

Fielding, Steve, *Cheshire Murder Casebook*, Countryside Books, 1996
Cheshire Chronicle

5. THE MAN OF BANGOR

PRO, HO 144/286/B298
Birkenhead News

Cheshire Chronicle
Liverpool Courier
Liverpool Daily Post
Standard
Hansard

6. 'MURDER LANE'

Evans, Stewart P., *Executioner – The Chronicles of James Berry*, Sutton, 2004
Yarwood, Derek, *Outrages – Fatal and Other*, Didsbury Press, 1991
Liverpool Courier
Liverpool Post
The Times

7. THE GORSE HALL MYSTERY

Fielding, Steve, *Cheshire Murder Casebook*, Countryside Books, 1996
Goodman, Jonathan, *The Stabbing of George Harry Storrs*, Allison & Busby, 1983
Lane, Brian, *Murder Club Guide to North West England*, Harrap, 1988
Murder Casebook Vol. 129, Marshall Cavendish, 1992
Daily Telegraph
Evening Reporter
Manchester Guardian
Stalybridge Times
Sunday Express

8. THE JILTED BOYFRIEND

Fielding, Steve, *Cheshire Murder Casebook*, Countryside Books, 1996
Macclesfield Courier & Herald

9. THE PHILANDERER

PRO, ASSI 65/22/3
Fielding, Steve, *Cheshire Murder Casebook*, Countryside Books, 1996
Liverpool Weekly Courier

10. THE LOSER

PRO, ASSI 65/27
Eddleston, John J., *Murderous Manchester*, Breedon Books, 1997
Cheshire Chronicle
Liverpool Echo
Observer (Cheshire)

11. THE CHINESE MYSTERY

PRO, ASSI 65/30/3
Marjoribanks, Edward, *The Life of Sir Edward Marshall Hall*, Cedric Chivers Ltd, 1929
Spencer Shew, E., *A Companion to Murder*, Cassell, 1960
Youd, Percy, *Tales from a Sporting Life*, Léonie Press, 2003
Murder Casebook Vol. 86, Marshall Cavendish, 1991
Daily Courier
Liverpool Echo

12. A FARMHOUSE TRAGEDY

PRO, ASSI 65/30/2
Fielding, Steve, *Cheshire Murder Casebook*, Countryside Books, 1996
Cheshire Courier
Liverpool Echo
Chronicle

13. DEATH ACROSS THE DEE

PRO, ASSI 65/32/1
Observer (Cheshire)

FURTHER READING

Dearden, Harold, *Some Cases of Bernard Spilsbury and Others*, Hutchinson, 1934
Eddleston, John J., *The Encyclopaedia of Executions*, John Blake, 2002
Morant, Roland W., *Cheshire Churches*, Countryvise [sic], 1989
Woodley, David, *Knutsford Prison – The Inside Story*, Léonie Press, 2002

INDEX